GW01571684

# A Brief History of
# King's

Text: Vivien Cripps
Drawings: Robin Hidden
Decorations: Roger Newton

Millrace

First published in Great Britain in 1997 by
Millrace
2a Leafield Road, Disley
Cheshire SK12 2JF

Text & illustrations © 1997 Millrace

ISBN: 1 902173 00 7

Printed and bound in Great Britain
by Antony Rowe Ltd, Chippenham, Wilts

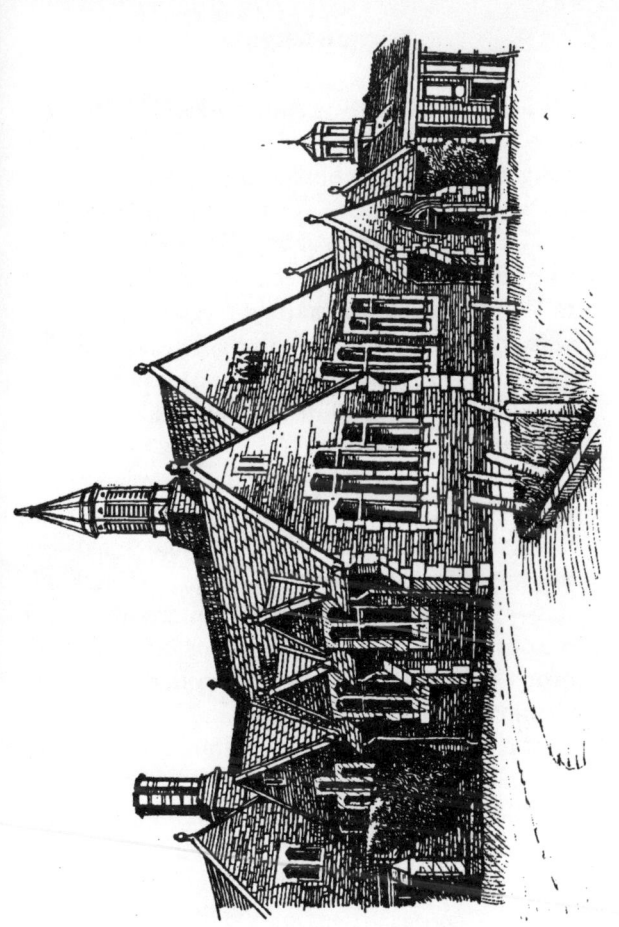

# Acknowledgments

Without the scholarly groundwork of G E Wilson, who in 1952 wrote a thesis on the history of the King's School, this book would have been far harder to write. I also owe a considerable debt to C S Davies for her absorbing *History of Macclesfield.* The works of G Malmgreen, P McGuinness and D Wilmot (see bibliography) were further valuable sources of information. I am grateful to the University of Nottingham Library for permission to quote from Sir William Meredith's letter to the Duke of Portland.

I have had so much help from so many people at King's. It is hard to know who to single out for thanks but I would especially like to express my appreciation to A S Haresign for his kindness in providing quantities of information and encouragement, M Patey-Ford for being so generous with his desk-top publishing expertise, K Aikin for keeping a professional historian's eye on the manuscript, the school librarians for their patience and help and, finally, the headmaster, A G Silcock, for giving permission for the project to go ahead and for taking a great interest in it. It has been fun.

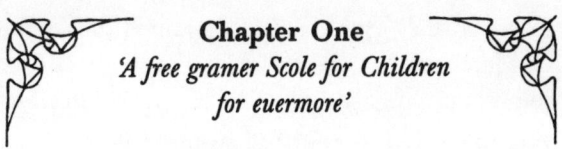

# Chapter One
## 'A free gramer Scole for Children
## for euermore'

Did Sir John Percvyale have any notion, when the trust deeds were drawn up in 1502, that his school in Macclesfield would still be flourishing nearly five hundred years later? He knew the uncertainty of life: he had, after all, lived through the upheavals of the Wars of the Roses. The murder of two kings and the death on Bosworth Field of a third had shown the folly of putting one's trust in princes. Yet he stipulated that his planned chantry school for teaching 'Gentilmens sonns and other good mennes Children of the Towne & Contre' should be 'for euermore'.[1]

Evidently he was an optimist. He was also a pragmatist. An able administrator himself, he would have recognised Henry VII's abilities and perhaps believed - ironically, as it turned out - that in the safe hands of the Tudors his fledgling school's chances of survival were good.

Born of obscure parentage somewhere near Macclesfield ('Maxfeld ... fast by the which Towne

I was borne'[1] ) John Percyvale joined the Guild of Merchant Taylors in London in 1450. It was the start of a highly successful career. Within eight years he was a freeman of the City of London. By 1486, the year after the death of Richard III, he had risen to become Master of his Guild, as well as Sheriff and Carver for the Lord Mayor. His knighthood was awarded in 1487 and in 1498 he became Lord Mayor of London.[2]

At some stage in this remarkable life, Sir John found time to win an equally remarkable wife. Thomasina Bonaventure began life in Cornwall as the child of poor parents, 'but not so poor but that her father had a small flock of sheep that depastured on the wastrell of Wike St Mary … whereof she was the shepherdess'. A passing London tradesman, Thomas Bumsby, was struck by her beauty and fell into conversation with her. Finding 'her discreet answers suitable to the beauty of her face', he bore her off to London to be his servant and, when his wife died, married her. Within two years Thomasina was a wealthy young widow, a prize quickly snapped up by Henry Galle, an 'eminent and wealthy citizen'. By the time she was thirty, Galle had also died, leaving her 'a richer widow than he found her'. By then her 'fame, virtue, wealth and beauty... spread itself in the city of London, so that persons of the greatest magnitude for wealth and dignity there courted her and amongst the rest, it was the fortune of John Percivale, Esq, to prevail with her to become his wife'.[3]

When, therefore, at the end of his life, Sir John turned his attention to founding a school, he was a rich and influential man, with a circle of powerful friends and a wealthy wife, who herself was to endow a school in Cornwall. He was part of the new moneyed merchant and middle classes who were to follow the nobles' long-established lead in setting up small chantry schools. Sir John was encouraged in his venture by his friends, Thomas Savage, Archbishop of York, and Sir Richard Sutton of Prestbury.

The Savages, established in Macclesfield in the middle of the fifteenth century, had married into the Stanley family. Sir John Savage's wife Catherine was the sister of Thomas Stanley, who had been granted the Stewardship of Macclesfield Forest by Richard III but transferred his allegiance to Henry VII at the Battle of Bosworth.

Shakespeare pinpoints the moment: 'What says Lord Stanley? Will he bring his power?' demands Richard III, only to hear the reply: 'My lord, he doth deny to come.' For this denial Stanley was rewarded with the earldom of Derby and the family became one of the most powerful in England.[4]

Catherine and Sir John Savage had ten sons, the second of whom was Sir John Percyvale's 'synguler good lord Thomas Archebisshop of york'[1]. Thomas Savage had himself planned to establish a collegiate school in Macclesfield but agreed to sell the land he had acquired to Sir John. Instead he built and endowed the Savage Chapel on the south side of the Church of All Hallows (now St Michael's) which had been founded by Queen Eleanor in 1278. He was generous to his friend's foundation: a further deed in 1504 conveyed 'lands in Mottram St Andrew area from Archbishop Savage'.[5]

Sir Richard Sutton, the other friend who provided Sir John with 'good & holsome Counsell'[1], was a member of Henry VII's Privy Council. In 1509 he was to co-found Brasenose College, Oxford, with statutes stipulating that preference should be given 'especially to the natives of the parish of Prescot in Lancashire and Prestbury in Cheshire' when choosing the Principal and Fellows.[6] The school in Macclesfield would also benefit under his will.

What was Macclesfield like at the beginning of the sixteenth century? Sir John Percyvale certainly considered it in urgent need of a school, for 'god of his haboundaunt grace hath sent and daily sendeth to the inhabitants there Copyous plentie of Children ... and vertue right fewe Techers and scolemaisters'.[1] The town had been slowly growing since the time when, as a small village, it had been given as part of the earldom of Chester to William the Conqueror's nephew. The Crown later reclaimed the earldom and in 1261 Macclesfield was granted a charter by Edward I, confirming it as a free Borough.[7] A royal demesne was built and visited several times by Edward I and Queen Eleanor. Later enlarged, it provided the Black Prince with a valuable source of income and a breeding ground for war horses, but by the fifteenth century the land was let and direct royal interest ceased.[8]

The mediaeval town itself was very small. At the end of the fourteenth century John de

Macclesfield, a royal favourite at the court of Richard II, built himself a castellated mansion at the top of Souter Lane (Backwallgate). The mansion passed to his son and then came into the hands of the Staffords, Dukes of Buckingham. Though it was let by the end of the fifteenth century, it was owned by the Staffords until the late sixteenth century, when the Earls of Derby took possession.[9] The Savage family mansion, Worth Hall, stood in the middle of Chestergate.

In the surrounding countryside there were clear signs early in the Tudor period that land was increasingly being cultivated, with about half the forest being occupied by settlers. Farms with sheepfolds and fields had been established and at Gawsworth, Bosley, Wincle and elsewhere enclosures had been made and cottages built. The town started to profit from increased trade as goods from the new farms were brought in to sell at the market. [10]

This was the setting in which Sir John Percyvale proposed to establish his 'free gramer Scole'. ('Free' probably meant an exemption from Mortmain, a mediaeval statute designed to prevent landowners evading feudal dues.[11]) It was the first school to be founded by a member of the Guild of Merchant Taylors, though not, of course, the last.[12] It was not the first school in the area. Edward Downes of Pott Shrigley, who died in 1494, had provided in his will for a school to be run by the priest of Pott Chapel. Downes stipulated that the priest should keep 'noe Horse, ne Hawke, ne Hounde' for fear he should not 'tend his book, ne writyng, ne teacyng of children ne his beades, ne other vertuous occupation'.[11] How to bind schoolmasters to a strict attendance of their duties was a question which would exercise the governors of the Macclesfield Grammar School on more than one occasion over the following centuries.

The governors of Sir John's new school were named as 'Edward ffyton of Goesworth, Rauf Damport [Davenport] of Damport, William Damport of Bromall, Thomas Hyde of Norburye, John Sutton of Sutton thelder & John his Eldest Son, Roger a leigh [Legh] thelder of the Rygge [Ridge Hall, Sutton] & Roger his Eldest Son, John Bridgis of Edgeley, Reignold Oldfield & John his Eldest Son, John worth of Tetrynton [Tytherington] the elder and John his Eldest Son,

Thomas Sherygley of Beyrystowe [Beristall Hall, near Pott Shrigley] the elder and Thomas his Eldest Son, Roger Rowe and Richard his Eldest Son'.[1] Most were local landowners. Rauf and William Damport were kinsmen of Mr William Bromley-Davenport, the present chairman of the board of governors.

These seventeen governors were charged 'to fynde & systeyn a vertues preest conyng in gramer & graduate' to act as schoolmaster and priest. His scholars were to join him in daily psalms and prayers for the souls of Sir John, his wife, Richard Sutton and 'for all xpen [Christian] Souls'. They were also expected to behave decorously in church, 'to syng & to say their s'uices wele and vertuously w'out Janglyng or talkyng or other Idell occupacion'.[1]

The school was set up close to the church. In those days the river Bollin ran through a wooded gorge and the drop from the high ground on which the church and school stood would have been much steeper than it is now. To the east, beyond the river, was the open common.[13] A deed of 1544 describes the school as 'a tenement with a garden to same, adjacent le Walgate, between the chapell of All Saints ... on the West part and the water of Macclesfield on the East'.[14]

William Bridges was the first master, appointed in 1502-3 and believed to have had his living quarters in two rooms above the Savage Chapel. He was a relative of Sir John Percyvale, who expressed complete confidence in 'the sadde disposicion & conyng of my kynnesman maister'[1] and he remained in office until his death thirty-five years later.

About ten years after his appointment, Macclesfield was called upon to help the northern shires repel an invader. The Scots had seized on the absence in France of Henry VIII to pour across the Tweed into Northumberland. Though the English won the Battle of Flodden, both sides suffered great losses and many Macclesfield men, including most of the leading burgesses, were killed.[15] The effect on the town was devastating.

Of William Bridges' pupils, the only one of whom there is any record is Raufe Holynzed, mentioned in Bridges' will as the beneficiary of 6s.9d and a horse.[16] This Raufe may have been the chronicler Holinshed, born about 1520 and thought to have been a native of Sutton, near

Macclesfield.[17] His *Chronicles of England, Scotland and Ireland* were used by Shakespeare as source material. Though none of Bridges' other pupils is mentioned by name, he planned that they should all, singers and non-singers, be rewarded for attending his funeral. 'I wyle that every scholere resorting to the Grammer Schole in Macclesfield them that can synge have ijd [2d] and every other of them to have jd[1d].'[16]

The last years of William Bridges' life witnessed the unfolding of a long-running royal drama: Henry VIII's extreme measures to procure a legitimate son, his break with the Church of Rome, the birth of Elizabeth and the despatch within three years of her mother to the executioner's block. The Macclesfield schoolmaster did not, however, live to see the legal devices which were to threaten the destruction of Sir John Percyvale's foundation before it had reached its first half-century: the Chantries Acts.

## Chapter Two
### *'A fair free School founded long since'*

It is not known who was master of the school during the decade between William Bridges' death and the visit to Macclesfield by Edward VI's Commissioners in 1548. Charles Alexander and Randall Pykerynge are the mostly likely candidates. Both were priests at All Hallows Church; either may have been in charge of the town's 'oon gramer scole' mentioned by the Commissioners.[1]

The visit had disturbing implications. Henry VIII's break with the Church of Rome had enabled him to embark on a highly profitable programme of stripping the Church of its wealth. He began with the monasteries. By 1545 he had turned his attention to the chantries but, before the Commissioners appointed under the first Chantries Act could complete their investigations, he died. The process he had begun did not. A new Act under Edward VI in 1547 abolished chantries and a great many chantry schools perished. Damned as a 'Scole in Decay', Thomasina

Bonaventure's school in Wike St Mary was among those to be closed.[2]

For a time the future of Sir John Percyvale's school hung in the balance. That it escaped the fate of his wife's was owing to two circumstances. The first was that both school and chantry were established at the same time: under the 1547 Act, schools attached to chantries could only continue if the school was mentioned 'in the first foundation and ordinance'.[3] The second was the strength of local feeling and influential support. According to a letter written years later by the governors to the Earl of Leicester, the re-foundation was achieved 'at the speciall travell, instance and medyacon of the late Duke of Northumberland, your honors father being thereunto moved at the humble sute of one Edmunde Sutton then his servant'.[4] Edmund Sutton was the nephew of Sir John Percyvale's friend, Richard Sutton

In the three years between the Commissioners' visit and the granting of a Continuance Warrant, the school was probably closed. On 26th April 1552, however, King Edward VI's Charter confirmed that 'henceforth there may and shall be one Grammar School in Macclesfield aforesaid which shall be called the Free Grammar School of King Edward the Sixth'.[5] The school's future was assured.

The re-foundation process brought with it some decided benefits. Not only did the school have its lands returned to it but it was also granted lands from the suppressed College of St John in Chester. The severing of the direct link with the Church meant a lessening of religious control, even if the conditions laid down in the Charter marked a beginning of State interference. There was no longer a requirement for the master to be a priest. Indeed, there would not be another clergyman-master until the time of the Restoration.

While far-reaching powers were given to the Bishop of Chester, Sir John Percyvale's original seventeen governors were reduced to a corporate body of fourteen. Their Common Seal - a silver one - is still in the school and its oval design of a scholar with a rod in one hand and a book in the other appears on the Bursar's stationery. Several of the surnames of the 'discrete and honest inhabitants' named as trustees are familiar from the 1502 list. The fourteen were: Edward Fytton of Gawsworth, John Davenport of Henbury, Richard Sutton of Sutton Hall, Robert Hyde, Jasper Worth of Worth, John Cresswell, James Broster, Hugh Hollynshead, Thomas Grene, John Henshaw, Roger Rowe, Thomas Stapulton, Thomas Marler and William Heyley. [6] All governors were expected to reside 'within the Vill of Macclesfield and Parish of Prestbury' - a requirement which was later to cause a major quarrel between them.

So, wealthier, reorganised and given new permanence by the Charter - for in future changes to the foundation could only be made by Act of Parliament - the school continued at its former site. It was to remain there until 1748. The value of its lands now amounted to £21.5s.0d a year, of which £1.5s.0d was to be paid to the Crown. [7]

Edward VI died before the school re-founded in his name could appoint a new master. John Bolde, a 'discrete man and skilled in grammar', took up the post in the first year of Queen Mary's reign. He was allowed 'the Schoole House with all the rooms to the said house belonging [and] the Schoole Bank' and a salary of £13.6s.8d. These benefits were his for life, provided he conducted himself with due decorum: 'If it shall happen that the said John Bolde shall become immoral or drunken or not discharge the said office or ... be absent ... more than six weeks in one year (except only on account of some illness) then the grant ... shall be void'.[8]

Such fears of lax behaviour may have been a reflection of the state of affairs discovered in Macclesfield and elsewhere in the area by the Catholic Bishop of Chester, Cuthbert Scott. Appointed by a queen intent on restoring the Roman Catholic religion, regardless of human cost, he reported indignantly on the situation in his diocese. Churches and chapels were disgracefully neglected, with livestock allowed to wander in and out, non-attendance at services was widespread, and immorality, drunkenness and brawling were on the increase.[9] Perhaps people had become sceptical after years of trimming their religious beliefs according to royal whim. They might soon have to change them again. If Mary's reign was bloody, it was also mercifully short and in 1558 Elizabeth I came to the throne.

Macclesfield had produced no martyrs during the years of religious change, concentrating instead on an unhurried process of growth and development. Now, in Elizabeth's reign, it began to show its increased prosperity in a flurry of re-building. The church was enlarged and a new Guildhall built. In the streets next to the market-place small warehouses sprang up for the button making trade. Later, a Royal Charter was granted, establishing the Barnaby Fair.

John Bolde survived only two years into this new reign. In 1560 he was succeeded by John Brownswerde, whose fame as a teacher, scholar and poet was to spread. Educated at Oxford and Cambridge, he was a native of Northwich. Over thirty years after his death, William Webb wrote of the school:

'There is also a fair free School founded long since, which about the beginning of Q *Elizabeths* happy reign, had a School-master of great fame for Learning and singular method of Teaching, who living many years, brought up most of the Gentry of this Shire; his name was *John Brounswerd*, stiled by most men that knew him, *Grammaticus.*'[10]

A memorial brass put up by his pupil, Tho-mas Newton, in the Legh Chapel of the parish church also styles him 'first of poets, chief among grammarians, flower of pedagogues'. He remained at the school for twenty-eight years, retiring shortly before his death in 1589, but his service may have been interrupted. According to an article written early this century, he abandoned Macclesfield for a few years to become master first at Warwick School and then at Stratford-upon-Avon. Research[11] suggests that his former schoolmaster, John Bretchgirdle, arranged the posts for him. As vicar of Stratford upon Avon, Bretchgirdle baptised the infant William Shakespeare in 1564, while Shakespeare's father, one of the burgesses involved with the Stratford school, is credited with helping Brownswerde with his removal expenses from Warwick to Stratford, where his first son was born in 1566.

There are, however, no known records in Macclesfield to support the idea either of Brownswerde's absence or his return in 1567. Nor is there any evidence of a replacement being appointed during that period, though there is a tradition that his pupil, Thomas Newton, taught for a time at the school.[12]

This pupil, Thomas Newton, was to become even more distinguished a man of letters than his teacher. Born in 1542, the eldest of fourteen children of a yeoman farmer in Butley, he left the school to go to Cambridge. From 1568 until his death in 1607 his output as a celebrated writer and poet[13] ranged from English and Latin verses to historical, medical and theological articles. In 1581 he published *Seneca His Tenne Tragedies*, which was to have a great influence on the Elizabethan playwrights.[14] It was a gifted age. Hilliard's miniatures, Marlowe's plays, the poems of Edmund Spenser and Sir Philip Sidney, the music of William Byrd were all part of a great flowering of the arts.

There were other kinds of tragedy and triumph. In 1587, Mary Queen of Scots was executed. A year later, the year Brownswerde retired, the Spanish Armada was defeated. The master who took over had no appetite for war. William Legh 'preferred to bear any injury rather than inflict one'.[15] His span of office, which began fifteen years before Elizabeth's death, outlasted the reign of James I and ran five years into that of Charles I.

Approved of by the governors 'as well for his discrete and honeste behavyour as for his knowledge in learninge',[16] William Legh taught Latin, Greek and Hebrew and was also skilled in Spanish, French and Italian. This was a time when Latin Grammar was the most important subject studied in schools, followed by Greek. Religion and morals also received attention, for the Tudors insisted on their particular brand of religion being taught in the grammar schools.[17]

Little else is known of William Legh. His name appears in an unexpectedly domestic connection on a document listing turbary rights - the right to cut peat for fuel. One of Macclesfield's privileges, dating back to the 1261 Charter, is to be allowed to cut peat on Danes Moss. Among the names of burgesses or commoners granted this right in 1611 is 'Mr Legh for the Schoolhouse ... 1 rood'.[18]

Occasionally news must have filtered through to the school of some of the social, political and literary events, momentous and trivial, that occurred during this period. While a stream of new plays by William Shakespeare appeared at the Globe, King James inveighed against the tobacco habit and Guy Fawkes plotted a different sort of combustion; while John Donne turned from seductive poems to sermons, the Crown offered hereditary titles for cash and the Mayflower settlers turned their back on Old World corruption. All were distant events which would have had little impact on the lives of the inhabitants of Macclesfield. The plague, which visited the town in 1602-3, was a different matter.

The seriousness of the situation was quickly recognised by the authorities and they hurried to contain the infection. 'Watch and ward was Kept at every common passage out of the towne and at crosse lanes near adjoining to ye towne to keep in ye Townsmen.'[19] Mortality was high, as the plague made its grim progress through the town via Dog Lane and Back Street, Chestergate and Mill Street. Poorer areas like the Gutters, the district behind the parish church, were the worst affected.[20] In just one month, from early September to early October 1603, over seventy people died, including nine members of one family. In the town's population of three to four thousand, there were a hundred and thirty deaths.[21]

## Chapter Three
### 'To bringe uppe institute and instruct children'

William Legh, the 'lover of peace',[1] died in 1630, spared the knowledge of the forthcoming confrontations between King and Parliament which would end in civil war. His statue lies in the Savage Chapel.

His replacement, Thomas Bold, was a Royalist, a 'man of learninge, discretion and good carryage'. Previously master of a school in Middlewich, he was elected in January 1631 'to bringe uppe institute and instruct children and youth in Grammar and goode literature'.[2] He and his wife also brought up five children of their own. The number of pupils increased, too. For the first time, there is a record of an assistant master, or usher - Hugh Normansell - who was appointed to teach the younger children.[3]

While the school prospered, the situation in the country became increasingly grave. In August 1642, King Charles I raised the royal standard at Nottingham and in October the first major battle of the Civil War was fought at Edgehill. The outcome was indecisive. By December, both sides had realised that the war would not be over quickly. Macclesfield, lying in a swathe of Parliament-held land between two Royalist areas, was involved in some early skirmishes. So, too, were many connected with the school.

While the Parliamentary forces were preoccupied with the siege of Nantwich, a former pupil of the school, Sir Thomas Aston, seized Macclesfield for the King. It did not take the Parliamentarians long to react and at the beginning of February 1643 they attacked and occupied the town. Colonel Legh of Adlington, a governor of the school and a Royalist, hurried to Macclesfield with a considerable force. There he was confronted by Colonel Mainwaring of Kermincham Hall, father of two boys in the school. Colonel Mainwaring 'with the assistance of the Countrey, did dryve him thence and hee disgysed in a Soldyers habit escaped. But his Drummer and more of those of his soldyers were theire slayn.'[4]

Colonel Mainwaring then turned his attention to Adlington Hall. Colonel Legh was away with the Royalist forces and, after a fortnight's siege, the Hall surrendered. Other country houses in the area also fell, leaving north-east Cheshire in Parliamentary hands.[5] Sir Thomas Aston, whose inexperienced troops proved quite unable to cope with the enemy in Cheshire, was withdrawn to Oxford and died of wounds in March 1645.[6]

Meanwhile, despite being a Royalist, Thomas Bold was allowed to remain in his post at the school. The three years before his death in 1645 cannot have been easy, with the tensions within the school mirroring those without, and news arriving of the crushing royal defeats at Marston Moor and Naseby. At least he did not live to see his king beheaded.

Henry Crosedale, the schoolmaster from Knutsford who replaced Bold, was, naturally, a Puritan, chosen by governors of mainly Parliamentary sympathies.[7] Within four years, Parliamentary power was confirmed when King Charles I was brought to trial and condemned to death. The president of the High Court of Justice was John Bradshaw. Born near Marple and thought to have been educated at Macclesfield Grammar School,[8] Bradshaw was later to take fierce issue with Cromwell for daring to dissolve

Parliament: 'Sir, you are mistaken to think that the Parliament is dissolved, for no power under heaven can dissolve them but themselves.' [9]

From 1649 both the Commonwealth Parliament and Cromwell were to invest much energy in trying to establish a sound national educational policy. Among other measures, grammar schools were required to give financial aid to enable impoverished students to go to university. Between 1654 and 1657, the governors of Macclesfield Grammar School made two grants of £10 and two of £20 'to Mr Crosedale for and towards the breeding of his sonne at the University'.[10] It is the first recorded scholarship at the school.

Other matters demanded the governors' attention during the Protectorate. One of the side-effects of the Civil War had been to prevent proper supervision of the school's lands in Chester. Although Sir John Percyvale's original foundation deed had specified the appointment of a 'rentgaderer', there was no such requirement in the re-foundation and the master and usher had to act as estate manager and clerk.[11] In a dispute which would drag on for some years, with Margaret Bold, widow of Thomas, being called as a witness for the school, the Chester tenants challenged the amount of rents claimed. Eventually, but not until after the Restoration, the matter was settled in the school's favour.

The coronation of Charles II was everywhere marked with lavish celebrations. In Macclesfield the corporation provided trumpeters, fireworks and 106 gallons of beer.[12] Such national rejoicing, however appropriate in other areas, was not justified where schools were concerned. The new government's interest in education extended only to ensuring that schoolmasters conformed to the Church of England and grammar schools were soon considered possible breeding grounds for sedition.[13] In 1662, the Puritan Henry Crosedale was turned out of his post for non-subscription to the Thirty-Nine Articles and was given £100 for relinquishing all claims on the school.

In his place came the Revd Edward Powell, the first master since the re-foundation to be a clergyman. That year Macclesfield was visited by a tornado, vividly described in an account published twenty years later:

'In the Forest of Maxfeld ... there arose a great pillar of smoke, in height like a steeple and judged twenty yards broad, which making a most hideous noise, went along the ground six or seven miles, and carried the stones a great distance from their places ... It went up by a Town called Taxal and thence to Waily Bridge where, and no where else, it overthrew an house or two ... From thence it went up into the hills of Derbyshire and so vanished.'[14]

At some stage in his first year, Powell displeased the governors. The offence remains a mystery but in April 1663 he wrote to them, pleading his cause:

'Before I went from home, I had the promise of a Gentleman ... to make my apologye, but I perceive it fayld; yet you will finde there was more unhappinesse than wilfulnesse in my offense, and that there was rather error than fault in the defect of my promise.'[15]

Whatever he had done, numbers at the school were healthy. A month later, he was reporting that his assistant master, John Legh, had more 'petty schollers' than he could attend to and the governors agreed to appoint Thomas Normansell to help him.[16] The petty school served as a kind of preparatory class, where pupils were taught

English, writing and simple arithmetic before entering the Grammar School proper.[17]

Powell died at the end of 1666, the first of three masters in succession to die after only a short time in office. In London that year up to 100,000 inhabitants perished in the Great Plague. Of those that remained, thousands were made homeless the following year by the Great Fire.

Ralph Gorst, of Christ's College, Cambridge, and master of Winwick School in Lancashire, was appointed to take William Powell's place. In 1671 he married a Macclesfield girl, Sarah Nickinson, but the marriage was tragically short. They died within a month of each other in 1674. Little else is known of him except that he 'did buy two seates in the Lower end of the front pew in the new gallery erected in the east end of the p'ochiall Chappell of Macclesfield'.[18] His nephew, Thomas Gorst, who inherited the seats, sold them to Edward Watson of Swanscoe for £4.4s.

The academic achievements of the Revd Thomas Brancker, who took over from Gorst, rivalled those of John Brownswerde a century earlier. He was born in Devon in 1635 and had been a fellow of Exeter College and rector of Tilston in

Cheshire. A preacher with Puritan tendencies, his interests were mainly scientific, although he was 'well skilled in the sacred and other languages'. He was 'a high authority and student of natural philosophy, Mathematics and Chemistry',[19] had written mathematical and scientific works and studied under Robert Boyle, of gas law fame.

By the time of Brancker's appointment in 1674, the school's endowment had increased from £21.5s in 1552 to about £140[20] and his salary was set at £31.8s. One of his more unusual duties was the inspection of a salt mine owned by the school in Nantwich. His report to the governors on 'the wallings of salt that belong to Macclesfield Schole' explains in detail the complex arrangements at the pit. The report found favour with the governors, who wrote to him expressing their entire satisfaction.[21]

Within eighteen months Thomas Brancker was dead, having been at the school for less than two years. In December 1679, the governors voted a form of pension to his widow, the first record of any such payment: 'that Mrs Brancker ... have five pounds paid to her for this yeare and fifty shillings yearely for seaven yeares next, if she so

long live, towards the payment of her house rent.'
She evidently did so long live for in 1687 it was
decided that 'Mrs Brancker be allowed fifty shillings at the Governors' pleasure'.[22]

It was while the next master, the Revd John
Ashworth, was at the school that its first library
was founded in 1681. It was set up largely thanks
to the efforts of a former pupil of the school, the
Revd Joshua Walker, and a bequest of £5 from
the Revd Robert Barlow towards 'furnishing up
a Library for the free Grammar Schoole at
Macclesfeelde'.[23] Ashworth himself contributed
a large number of volumes. The books - about
two hundred - are listed in a beautifully written
catalogue, giving edition, donor and date.[24] Alas,
none appears to be in the Library today.

Before coming to Macclesfield in 1676, John
Ashworth had been master of the Merchant
Taylors' School in Crosby. From 1684 to 1689,
he also acted as perpetual curate in Macclesfield.
At the start of that period, Charles II granted a
charter to the town. As well as establishing two
more annual fairs, it authorised the corporation
to carry water 'in or through pipes or otherwise'
from the Common to the town. Since the water

from the town's well was described as 'noisesome and pernicious' and the steep hill down to the Bollin made the river an inconvenient supply, this was a great advantage. Later, the plentiful source of soft water from the Common would prove invaluable as Macclesfield's textile industry developed.[25]

A year after granting the charter, Charles II died, survived only five months by his illegitimate son. The Duke of Monmouth, who in 1682 had stayed in Gawsworth at the home of Sir Richard Legh, was beheaded on Tower Hill in July 1685. His attempt to seize the throne had been crushed at Sedgemoor. James II's triumph was brief; in 1688 he fled to France. In Macclesfield, John Ashworth lived just long enough to see William and Mary established on the throne. His death was to unleash a long and bitter battle between the governors over the appointment of a successor.

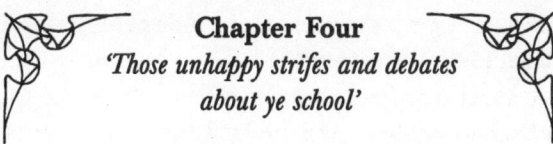

# Chapter Four

### *'Those unhappy strifes and debates about ye school'*

Despite the religious and social upheavals, wars and rebellions that had taken place since its re-foundation, the school had prospered. Numbers had increased and a reputation for sending students to the universities had been firmly established. The records of just one Cambridge college - St John's - list several entrants from Macclesfield Grammar School between 1637 and the end of the century,[1] and many boys from the school would have gone to other colleges. But in the final decade of the seventeenth century and the early part of the eighteenth the school's reputation was to plummet. The decline began with a protracted quarrel between the governors.

The root of the problem lay in the requirement in King Edward VI's Charter that the school governors should be resident 'in the Vill of Macclesfield and Parish of Prestbury'. By November 1689, when it came to appointing a new master, four of the governors had moved outside the parish. A decision was taken to disqualify these four, resulting in a split and the formation of two violently opposed parties, one led by Peter Legh, who had succeeded to the Lyme estate two years earlier, and the other by Edward Thorneycroft. Each party declared itself the rightful governing body and each put forward its own candidate to replace John Ashworth. The rivals were Timothy Dobson, master of Stockport Grammar School, and the Revd Caleb Pott, son of the vicar of Hurdsfield and half-brother of Joshua Walker, who had done so much towards founding the school's library.[2]

The governors seem to have forgotten altogether another requirement of the Charter, that they should be 'discreet and honest inhabitants', though discretion was certainly exercised later when the pages recording the election of the new master were ripped out of the minute book. Luckily, a lively contemporary account exists. While Peter Legh turned out five governors and replaced them with new ones to elect Caleb Pott, 'seven of ye old Governors went and Elected one Dobson … and accordingly went and put the said Mr D[ob]son into possession by giving him ye keys of ye Schol ... After this ye Governors went home, but great fraction these unjust dealings had made.' Greater fraction was to come. Timothy Dobson was unwise enough to leave the field briefly, leaving a substitute in charge, whereupon Legh's party seized their chance, 'came in riotous manner and pull'd out ye said Substitute by force ... pulled ye ould lock of and sett on a new one, likewise on ye Chamber above stairs'.[3] The Legh camp had triumphed, but only temporarily. Caleb Pott died in 1690.

His replacement, the Revd William Foxlowe, was a wealthy schoolmaster from Chesterfield. He remained in the post for less than a year before opening a private school in Macclesfield in order, as the Bishop of Chester put it, 'to draw schollers from ye publick school, to raise disturbance in ye town and to maintain those unhappy strifes and debates about ye school which have continued too long already'.[4] He had to be lured away with the promise of the living at Prestbury. At last, Caleb Pott's original rival, Timothy Dobson, could be appointed 'at the annual salary of Sixty Pounds, and that he have the School House, Schoole Banke, barn and Stable'.[5] He was to enjoy them until his death in 1704. At the same time the first clerk, Edward Cherry, was elected at £5 per annum. Masters would no longer have to supervise the school's estates.

When the governors' dispute was finally submitted to arbitration, Peter Legh's party was reprimanded for its conduct and made to pay the costs of the suits, totalling £1300. Legh himself had to pay £500.[6] The cost to the school of the controversy was considerable for the prolonged quarrel and the rapid turnover of masters had severely damaged its standing in the area.

The number of pupils at the school fell at a time when the population in Macclesfield was rising. Increased housing needs resulted in a new brick works being sited on the Common in 1696. The button making which had begun in the reign of Elizabeth I had by now become a significant cottage industry producing silk buttons and silk twist, with local merchants distributing the materials to their workpeople.[7] In 1698 a workhouse was set up to house poor children and to instruct them in the art of button making and spinning.[8]

In another twelve years, changes in fashion and the manufacture of cheap metal buttons in

Birmingham would cause a slump in demand for the silk variety. Fortunately, the skills which had been developed in the preparation and twisting of raw silk for buttons were transferable. Silk thread from Macclesfield would be sold in London, where the Huguenots had set up their looms in Spitalfields, and - for the time being at least - the operation would still mostly be carried out in the homes of the workpeople.[9] Later, with increasing industrialisation, the situation would change radically but, when the new master took over at the school in 1704, Macclesfield was still principally a market town. A new reign had begun two years earlier, with the accession of Queen Anne to the throne; the Duke of Marlborough was embarking on his series of famous victories and, with the Act of Union between England and Scotland, the United Kingdom of Great Britain was shortly to come into being.

Though Timothy Dobson's replacement, Edward Denham, would eventually cause even greater damage to the school's reputation than had the warring governors, his credentials on arrival at the school seemed impeccable. An Eton scholar, he had been awarded a BA at King's

College, Cambridge, in 1693, an MA in 1697 and had been a fellow of his college. His salary was £50 per annum, with £10 more 'at ye discretion of ye Governors',[10] and his future should have been promising. Yet, less than a dozen years later he was in gaol, awaiting trial for murder.

What caused his downfall? Little is known about him before his indictment for murder but it is clear from witnesses' statements that by 1716 he was regarded as a habitual drunkard. What is not clear is what drove him to this state. Being a bachelor, he did not live in the school house but lodged in chambers over the school. Two ushers are named as his assistants and his meals were provided by a Mrs Frances Ashworth - a courtesy title for she was unmarried - who lived in the adjoining school house.

Edward Denham's life seems to have been a solitary one: 'he conversed with nobody but the sd Mrs Ashworth and ... kept his chambers so close that many of the Townspeople scarce ever saw him; he did seldom appear at Church above thrice in a Year and his Comon Life was to Drink all night and lye in bed all Day and to drink in his bed so that he was scarce ever sober.'

Very late on the night of Friday 5th October 1716, after a bout of drinking lasting three days, Denham despatched his servant Jonathan Norbury to summon Mrs Ashworth to him. She resolutely refused to come until the morning, whereupon Denham 'with a Long Knife which he had concealed in his Gown, gave Norbury a wound in the Throat, Saying, take you that, go tell Mrs Ashworth I have cutt your throat upon her account.' Norbury was attended to by a surgeon but the wound was slight and he 'was cured the Same Night'. Meanwhile, Denham, still infuriated with Mrs Ashworth, rounded off his night's activities by discharging a pistol into her house. Four bullets lodged in the wall by the fireplace but she was unhurt.

When Francis Adshead, a pupil of Denham's who also acted as his servant, arrived at his chambers the following morning, he found the master drunk in bed. Denham was to despatch the boy to the alehouse several times during the day. At about five in the afternoon he got up but continued drinking, frequently sending the boy for further supplies. In between such errands, the boy had to take several notes to Mrs Ashworth. She ignored them all. 'At length Mr Denham sent Adshead to tell her to [take] care of herself and the rest of the family.' She immediately applied to the magistrates and, with their permission, hired three men to guard the house. Adshead, returning to Denham's chambers, saw that he had propped a gun against the chimney.

After overhearing the master refuse to accompany the sergeants sent by the Mayor, Adshead locked the outer chamber door and retired to Mrs Ashworth's. At about nine o'clock, he 'went out to see if Mr Denham had any light in his chamber and saw him coming att the School Door towards the School House with a candle in his hands'. Thomas Davie, one of the guards hired by Mrs Ashworth, ran to the school door. 'Mr Denham shut it … [but] opened it again and after some talk … pretended in his Gown for a Key and pulled out a Pistoll loaded with three bulletts and shot [him].' Thomas Davie 'then and there instantly Dy'd'.

Denham resisted arrest that night but an armed guard was set to prevent his escape. A neighbour, who had been drinking at Thomas Davie's home when news of the killing was brought, ran to the school. Finding Denham's door locked, he demanded to know who had killed Davie. 'The said Mr Denham answered, I have killed a villain and I am satisfied. And further saith noth.'

The following morning Denham gave himself up. Inside his rooms were found 'two Screw Pistolls lyeing upon the Table, loaded with powder and ball, his Sword drawn upon his desk, a flask of powder and a small Gun Loaden, lyeing by it, one paper of bulletts and another of flints lyeing open upon a Tea-Table.' He was taken to the Castle Gaol at Chester to await trial.

The indictment document 'supposed that the prisoner will plead Lunacy'. An odd note is appended: 'If Mrs Frances Ashworth appear as a witness pray examin her strictly and especially about his shooting into the house on fryday night.'[11] Was she garrulous and inclined to stray from the facts? Or was she too ready to try to excuse her employer? Whatever, she was not required to appear as a witness. Before he could be brought to trial, Edward Denham died. He was buried on 22nd April 1717.

The whole case had posed an unprecedented problem for the governors. Their first instinct on

Denham's arrest had been to dismiss him forthwith and appoint a successor but, after consideration, they resolved to await the outcome of the trial. George Hammond was appointed 'coadjutor in the said School during ... Mr Denham's incapacity'.[12] On Denham's death, he became master at a salary of £60 per annum and remained at the school until his resignation in 1720.

It has been commented that secondary education reached its lowest level in the eighteenth century[13]. Certainly Macclesfield Grammar School had reached its nadir. It would not be until the last quarter of the century that it would fully regain - and surpass - its previous good reputation.

# Chapter Five
### *'Surely his Grace never took me for a Jacobite?'*

I n the year that Charles Edward Stuart, the Young Pretender, was born, the Revd Joseph Allen, curate of Peover, became headmaster of the school. A quarter of a century later, his death would occur in the same year that the Young Pretender led his Jacobite army down from Scotland, calling at Macclesfield on the route south.

Open support for the Stuart cause was not advisable when Joseph Allen took up his post at the school in 1720. Since George I had been imported from Hanover six years earlier to ensure a Protestant monarchy, there had been Jacobite uprisings in Scotland and the north. Although they had been put down, the situation was still sensitive and it was a serious matter when the new headmaster's loyalty to the Hanoverians was called into question. On September 30th 1721, Allen wrote at some length to Lady Isabella Legh, wife of John Legh of Adlington, endeavouring to clear himself:

41

'I never heard any Gentleman in England ever declare himself more in favour of ye House of Hanover than ye Archbishop of York, and surely his Grace never took me for a Jacobite when he recommend me to ye Governors of Macclesfield. No, my Lady, and if any one ... will ev[idence] yt ever I shew'd a Dislike to ye Protestant Succession in ye House of Hanover, I will readily disclaim any Title to your Ladyship's Favour or any Persons upon Earth.'[1]

His arguments must have satisfied Lady Isabella and the governors, for he continued at the school and was also allowed to act as curate-in-charge at Capesthorne. When he died in April 1745, he was buried in the chapel yard there.[2]

During Allen's time at the school, the process which would transform Macclesfield into an industrial town began to gather pace. Earlier, in 1716, the lord of the manor of neighbouring Stockport had sold off common land as sites for factories and houses, ignoring the needs of those who depended on grazing land for their livelihoods. Now, in Macclesfield too, the common land was steadily being eroded. By 1740, buildings on the Common would include two silk works, a dyehouse, barns and stables, as well as a great number of houses, gardens and orchards. On the bank of the river Bollin, twenty-five acres of land, known as the Haleyfields and belonging to the Grammar School, were also enclosed.[3]

The town's population at this time was around 4,500[4] and suffered from various ailments. James Clegg, dissenting minister and 'Doctor of Physick' of Malcoff, gives an account of the diseases he had to treat in a practice which included Macclesfield. He mentions a variety of fevers, smallpox (which he treated with a powder of 'crabs eyes and oyster shells Levigated, sal prunella, Saffron and Bole armenian'), arthritic pains, rheumatic disorders, 'colic', 'pleuritick peripneumony', and 'chincough'. One patient was the daughter of Mr Thornley of Macclesfield, whose affliction with 'scrophulous swellings', he treated with 'the ethiops mineral and frequent purges and a dyet drink.'[5]

Perhaps it was the unhealthy climate that prompted the school governors to include in a new set of rulings one about absence through illness: 'If ye Head Master shall by a chronical distemper become incapable of attending ye School, the one Moiety of his salary shall from thence forth be allowed to ye person whom ye Trustees shall appoint [to replace him]'. These 'Articles to be Observed by the Head Schoolmaster'[6] were drawn up in 1745, in time for Joseph Allen's replacement. The governors evidently wished to ensure that earlier problems were avoided.

The Articles' first demand was for 'a bond to be entered into by ye master for performance'. Edward Ford, who was appointed after Joseph Allen's death, gave £5000, as did his successor, Christopher Atkinson, but the stipulation then seems to have lapsed. Another clause required the headmaster to give up any church living. Had Allen's curacy stopped him concentrating fully on the school? At the same time he must attend church regularly - as Edward Denham spectacularly had not - and 'instruct his scholars at least once every week in ye principles of religion'. The religion concerned was that of the Established Church. Determined to preserve orthodoxy, the governors stated that the master should resign 'if at any time it shall appear that [he] be an atheist, Deist, Arrian, Socinian or ... not Strictly Conformable to the Church of England'.

There were other articles concerning teaching hours and holidays. Between 'Candlemas and Michaelmas', the headmaster was expected to teach between seven in the morning and five in the evening, with a two-hour break for lunch. The hours for the Autumn-Winter session were shorter because of the reduced daylight, while holidays - at Whitsuntide and Christmas - 'should not exceed a month at any one time'. Nor should the Head Master be absent from school except on 'honest, necessary and reasonable business'. Finally, in a clear reference to an earlier dilemma, the governors stipulated that 'if ye Head Master be remiss or negligent in teaching ye Scholars, or be vicious, profane or guilty of any Crime … which may render him Scandalous … the said Master shall resign upon request.'

Was all this too daunting for the Revd Edward Ford? He resigned very shortly after his election, to be replaced in September 1745 by Christopher Atkinson, graduate of Queen's College, Oxford. Atkinson's brother, Rowland, became second master. The two men established themselves in Macclesfield just in time for the arrival of Bonnie Prince Charlie on his march south.

The Young Pretender had sailed for Scotland in July that year. Within a week of raising his father's standard, he had rallied an army of 2,000 Highlanders to the Stuart cause. After routing government forces at Prestonpans, he swept through northern England and, on 1st December, arrived in Macclesfield with an army of about 6,000 men and 500 cavalry. A small advance guard had reached the town the day before and tried unsuccessfully to recruit support. They also commandeered Sir Peter Davenport's house in Back Street (later King Edward Street) as living quarters for the Prince. The troops who followed them were 'very poorly mounted ... on such horses as they pickt up in the country as they came along, but many were lusty clever fellows ... The foot came in very regular order with Bagpipes playing instead of Drums ... and all the forces were in Highland dress'. The Prince, too, was 'in Highland dress with a blue waistcote trim'd with silver and had a blue Highland cap on ... a very handsome person of a man'.[7]

Despite all this splendour, the welcome from the people of Macclesfield was far from warm. Indeed, 'there was profound silence and nothing to be seen in the countenances of the Inhabitants but horror and amazement'. It was felt politic to greet the Prince with a peal of bells but only four ringers could be found 'and they rung the Bells backwards, not with design, but through confusion'.[7] The troops stayed in the town until 3rd December, appropriating all the arms, ammunition, corn, hay and provisions they could lay hands on and forcing the town's bakers to bake them wagon-loads of bread for their long march.

The lack of enthusiasm for the rebel cause was mirrored further south and when they reached Derby the decision was reluctantly taken to retreat. News of their return horrified the inhabitants of Macclesfield. Those who could, promptly took refuge with friends in the surrounding countryside; others barricaded themselves into their houses. The Prince did not return to the town, having ridden over the moors from Leek to Buxton, but the main body of the army arrived back in Macclesfield on Sunday 8th December.[8] John Stafford, Town Clerk, describes the events and their sequel in a letter to a friend:

'The officers on the whole behaved very well but the common soldiers behaved like devils, especially in their retreat, for they … pilfered and plundered people of their money, bedding, clothes and whatever they could carry away. On Tuesday last, December 10th, we were joyfully relieved by the arrival of the King's forces, under the command of the Duke of Cumberland, and his Royal Highness did me the honour of taking up his quarters at my home.'[9]

The Jacobite army was forced to return to the Highlands before the Duke of Cumberland's advance. By April 1746 all hope of deposing George II and returning a Stuart to the throne was over. The Highland army, hopelessly outnumbered, had been cut to ribbons at Culloden.

After the departure of the various forces, Macclesfield breathed a sigh of relief. John Stafford's house was renamed Cumberland House in honour of its royal guest and the town turned back to its usual affairs. For the school, however, a move was imminent. After two and a half centuries in the same buildings, next to a church that had recently undergone major restructuring, the governors felt that action was needed. They had already decided that the old school should be demolished and a new one built on the site[10] when

Sir Peter Davenport's house, the one briefly occupied by the Young Pretender, came on the
market. Abandoning their earlier plans, the governors bought it in July 1748 from Sir Peter's ex-
ecutors for £550. The old school was sold to a
local button merchant, Nathaniel Braddock, for
£120.[11]

Certain changes had to be made to turn the
gentleman's residence into a school. The marble
chimney pieces were sold; so, too, were the stalls
and furniture in the stable and the garden in front
of the house. Writing nearly seventy years later,
Ormerod described the site: 'The Grammar
School of Macclesfield ... is situated at the west
end of the town, in King Edward Street, and forms
with the school and various buildings (including
the residence of the head master) three sides of a
quadrangle.'[12] There the school would remain
for the next hundred years.

## Chapter Six
### *'Enlarging the Original Plan of the Royal Founder'*

Christopher and Rowland Atkinson, head master and second master at the time of the school's move to King Edward Street in 1748, were the sons of Miles Atkinson of Windermere.[1] Christopher Atkinson's rule was brief; the following year he resigned and the role was taken over by his brother. At the same time, a second Lake District connection was established with the arrival at the school of Adam Walker, son of a Troutbeck miller. His appointment as writing and accounts master shows how the school's curriculum was starting to expand.

Adam Walker was something of a mathematical genius. He was also a little odd. Local people muttered that he was in league with the devil and refused to have anything to do with him. When he left the school in 1753, it was to become a hermit on an island in Lake Windermere, but he later rejoined the outside world to lecture on scientific subjects. His reception this time was rather different. After a lecture in London had made him famous, he was invited to speak at Eton, Winchester, Rugby and St Paul's.[2] The contrasting attitudes he met with underline the co-existence of lingering mediaeval superstitions with a growing interest in science and technology.

One of the men who was to ensure that scientific and technological advances would be harnessed to increasing Macclesfield's - and his own - prosperity was Charles Roe, who became a leading figure in the town. The youngest son of the vicar of Castleton, he first came to Macclesfield in about 1740 and soon afterwards built a water-powered silk-spinning mill at Park Green. Other entrepreneurs copied his example.

Roe's ambitions were not limited to textiles. Nor, it seems, were those of the headmaster of the Grammar School to education. Rowland Atkinson had married Roe's sister Mary in 1748 and ten years later the two men went into partnership, founding the Macclesfield Copper Company: 'Mr Charles Roe and Mr Rowland Atkinson ... may have liberty to inclose forty yards square out of the waste lands in Macclesfield ... at or near a place on the Common called the

Highledge and erect thereon a smelting mill.'[3]
At least one of the school governors disapproved
of Atkinson's spirit of enterprise. Writing in 1774,
after the headmaster's death, Sir William
Meredith commented: 'The last master (tho' a
very bad one) had usually forty or fifty boarders,
as long as he gave the least attention to them, but
he soon got rich and put his money into trade.'[4]

The trade in question proved highly successful. The Copper Company paid its workmen with
trade tokens known as Macclesfield Pennies. John
Byng was given some of these coins at a turnpike
in Buxton: 'I was surprised to receive in change
the Anglesey and Macclesfield half-pence; a better coinage and of more beauty than that of the
Mint and not so likely to be counterfeited.'[5]

Whether a good headmaster or not, Rowland
Atkinson remained in office for nearly twenty-
five years, a period that saw the coronation of
George III and the publication of novels by
Richardson, Fielding and Smollett. While soci-
ety figures were being painted by Joshua
Reynolds and Thomas Gainsborough, the gov-
ernment was receiving the satirical attention of
John Wilkes' pen. Transport was improving with

the growth of the canal system and the spread of turnpike roads and, in Macclesfield in 1770, Charles Roe was the first person to acquire a private carriage. That same year a wooden playhouse was built in Chestergate. Though it attracted some notable companies, it also attracted hostility from the local clergy, who believed that 'one playhouse ruins more souls than fifty churches can save'.[6] It was forced to close down.

One of those to speak out against the playhouse was the Revd David Simpson, an Anglican with very strong Methodist sympathies. Methodism was flourishing in the area and John Wesley himself would later be invited by David Simpson to preach at Christ Church. This was the church built for Simpson in 1775 by Charles Roe, a close friend and supporter, after Simpson's outspoken preaching had made him some powerful enemies. One such was Sir William Meredith of Henbury Hall, Privy Councillor, Comptroller of the Royal Household and governor of the Grammar School. His importance did not prevent Simpson from using the pulpit of St Michael's to denounce his dissolute private life. Sir William took exception to this, complained to the Bishop and Simpson was advised to resign.[7] Soon afterwards he was installed in Charles Roe's brand new church, built on land purchased from the Grammar School.[8]

The sale of school land had been legalised by a Private Act of Parliament the year before. As early as the 1760s the governors had recognised that the school must adapt to the changing social and economic needs of the town and the first tentative steps had been taken by appointing masters to teach accounts and French. Now the Foundation, in a very healthy state financially, was in a good position to break out of the narrow classical curriculum imposed by the Charter of Edward VI. In 1773 the governors decided to apply for a Private Act 'for enlarging the Original Plan of the Royal Founder ... by adapting the same to the circumstances of the present times'.[9]

The Act was obtained in 1774 at a cost of £438.10s.0d. It regularised previous sales and purchases of land and allowed the governors to make further transactions and grant leases for a period of 99 years. More importantly, it authorised the appointment of masters 'to instruct the children and youth ... not only in grammar and classical learning, but also in Writing, Arithmetic, Geography, Navigation, Mathematics, the modern languages and other branches of literature and education'.[10]

It was an enlightened step for the governors to take. Though a few other grammar schools also acted to broaden the base of the education they offered, in the country as a whole grammar and public schools were in decline.[11] Sunday schools, on the other hand, were growing apace. Two schools for the poor, teaching children in the evenings, were started by the Revd Simpson in 1778, and in 1796 John Whitaker was to open a free Sunday school in Pickford Street.[12] Not everyone was convinced of the value of such schools. John Byng, visiting Stockport in 1790, remarks: 'I have met some [scholars] of the newly adopted Sunday Schools today … I am point blank against these institutions; the poor should not read, and of writing I never heard, for them, the use.'[13]

The name which appears on the 1774 Act of Parliament is that of the Revd Jennings, second master and temporary headmaster after Rowland Atkinson's death in 1773. The governors were looking for someone suitable to put their new scheme into practice. Sir William Meredith, an active governor whatever his private habits, went to London in search of such a man. In July 1774 he wrote that he 'liked none' of the Westminster-educated candidates who had been mentioned to him and was beginning to despair. Then he heard of the Revd Henry Ingles: 'An old School-fellow of his has shewn me some of his Compositions which are admirable and they say he is very well bred and much of a Gentleman.'[14] Ingles, a foundation scholar of Eton and fellow of Trinity College, Cambridge, was duly appointed in September 1774 at a salary of £100.

There was some confusion over the exact income provided by the post. The Duke of Portland seems to have proposed his own candidate, who evidently thought the income greater than it was. In a letter dated 20th July 1774, Sir William Meredith endeavours to make matters clear:

'There's an estate of about £700 a year, on which money was raised about 50 or 60 years ago, by granting Leases for Lives. There's £170 a year out of Leases, charged with £40 salary to an Usher, & a small Debt. We cannot at present afford more than 100 Guineas a year to the head

Master - with a very good house and field, the buildings always repaired at the Trust's expence.'[15]

Though he denies engaging 'to procure 50 boarders', he describes the possibilities of a situation 'where there are such prodigious numbers of opulent persons who want places of education for their children'.

The prospects were good and the Revd Inglis and his successor were to make the most of them. During the next fifty years the school's reputation soared and the chief families in Cheshire sent their boys there.[16] In the 1780s the three sons of General Sir Ralph Abercromby entered the school. The elder two boys were to have military careers like their father, who died of wounds after the Battle of Alexandria; the younger, James, became MP for Edinburgh, Judge Advocate General and a Master of the Mint. Created Lord Dunfermline in 1839, he was a Cabinet member in 1854 and Speaker of the House of Commons in 1855. Charles Lutwidge, who joined the school a few years before the Abercrombies, would be more famous for his grandson, Charles Lutwidge Dodgson, better known as Lewis Carroll, Oxford mathematician and author of *Alice*.

Ingles resigned in 1790. A stern disciplinarian, he was known at Rugby, where he became headmaster four years later, as the 'Black Tyger'. It was while he was there that the great rebellion of students took place, triggered by the flogging of a boy for purchasing gunpowder. Ingles himself was threatened with violence. The military were called in, the Riot Act read and a large numbers of boys flogged or expelled.

By contrast, the surface of his reign at Macclesfield was unruffled. On his resignation he was thanked by the governors for 'the great credit his exertions [had] gained the school at the universities'. Sixteen years earlier Sir William Meredith had written that he was convinced that 'a man of reputation would make the School we are speaking of, one of the greatest in England'.[15] Under Ingles' leadership and that of his successor, Dr Davies, the school did indeed acquire a very high profile.

## Chapter Seven
*'An able and learned headmaster'*

The first - and most successful period - of the Revd David Davies' lengthy headmastership coincided with the French Revolution and the Napoleonic wars. Contrary to their normal ruling, the governors patriotically allowed him to take on two extra roles. He became military chaplain to the Macclesfield Volunteers under Colonel Davies Davenport of Capesthorne and the Macclesfield Loyal Foresters under Jasper Hulley.[1]

Davies was to prove a worthy successor to Henry Ingles. He was a native of Machynlleth and a graduate of Jesus College, Oxford, and had already been at the school for eleven years as second master when he took over in 1790. An 'able and learned headmaster',[2] for twenty-five years he steered the school with vigour, making far-sighted suggestions to the governors regarding its organisation. It was not until the post-war period that his grip began to slacken.

At that time Macclesfield was undergoing rapid change and industrialisation. Silk weaving had just been introduced alongside the well-established spinning processes, and the silk trade was all set to prosper. Thanks to the war, French silk would be in no position to compete.[3] It was about this time, too, that the first Irish workpeople were arriving in the town to take advantage of the jobs available. John Byng visited Macclesfield in 1790 and commented on its prosperity:

'Macclesfield looks well in approach; and one knows a place to be enriching and increasing when it is surrounded by brick-kilns; the copper works have done this ... The remains of Macclesfield Castle have been pull'd down about twenty years and houses are built upon the ground. I put up at the Old Angel Inn and was happy to attack a boil'd buttock of a bull; hunger is not refined.'[4]

Two years later he returned to note the town's newly paved streets and the flourishing state of the silk and copper trades. He also visited 'Mr Roe's great copper works', which interested him but he felt that the workmen were poorly paid, as the best earned only fourteen shillings a week.[5]

Others in the town fared rather better. There was a great deal of prosperity in some quarters and the school, its reputation restored and enhanced, profited by it. Under Dr Davies, the numbers of boarders and day scholars increased. The first official census in 1801 gave a total population of 8743 in Macclesfield; by 1802 there were six classes in the school, composed of seventy-two boarders and nineteen day scholars. Even at the usual two or three to a bed, they cannot all have boarded in the school house. Parents who felt their sons should have the privilege of a single bed were charged an extra two guineas.[6]

A list - the first of its kind at the school - of all boys entering the school was compiled from 1775-1801 by Thomas Molineux, writing and arithmetic master and author of various textbooks. The 1792 entrants included James Parke, who was the Senior Chancellor's Medallist in 1803 and became Lord Wensleydale in 1856.[7] In 1794 John Ryle joined the school. With the Brocklehursts, the Ryles were one of the leading families of Macclesfield and John Ryle was to be one of the town's first MPs when Macclesfield was made a parliamentary borough in 1832.

A form of Old Boys' Society was already in existence. An advertisement in the *Morning Chronicle* on 19th September 1807 invited 'Gentlemen educated at Macclesfield School' to their annual meeting. Dinner would be on the table at 5 o'clock and 'those gentlemen who intend honouring the Stewards with their company' were requested to send their names as early as possible to Mr Browne.

The years between the victories at Trafalgar and Waterloo were coloured by a variety of events, local and national. The slave trade was abolished in Britain but children of all ages were still being exploited in factories and mines. A prime minister was assassinated, a king declared insane and his son made regent. The latter showed great interest in the novels of a new writer, Jane Austen. Science and technology were being advanced by John Dalton's new table of atomic weights, Michael Faraday's work on electricity and George Stephenson's locomotive, but the Luddites were doing their best to destroy the new textile-making machinery.

In Macclesfield, the inaugural issue of the town's first newspaper, *The Courier*, was brought out in 1811.[8] One of its early reports was on the opening of a new theatre, the Theatre Royal, in Mill Street. Elsewhere in the town, steam-driven mills were being built and in 1814, at the instigation of Dr Francis Newbold - whose son would later become headmaster of the Grammar School - a Town Dispensary was set up.

Two pupils who entered the school during this period were Brian Houghton Hodgson, later a distinguished zoologist and authority on Sanskrit, a Fellow of the Royal Society and Chevalier of the Legion of Honour, and George Long, who in 1830 was one of the founders of the Royal Geographical Society.[9]

With the victory at Waterloo in 1815, the prosperous era of the years of the French Wars ended and the silk industry entered a period of depression as demand for British silk fell. Manufacturers went bankrupt and returning soldiers joined the scramble for the remaining jobs; wages dropped to nearly half but the price of food remained high.[10] Poverty and suffering provoked the gradual politicisation of the work force. On the night of 15th August 1819 the radical orator Henry Hunt stayed in Macclesfield and addressed a large crowd on Park Green. He was on his way to the mass meeting, later to be known as Peterloo, at St Peter's Field, Manchester. As soon as news of the disastrous outcome of that meeting filtered through, a Macclesfield mob attacked the homes of wealthy Tories, including members of the Yeoman Cavalry.[11] John Wishaw, an old boy of the school, had first-hand news of the event: 'Smyth informed me that his family had a narrow escape at Macclesfield, the house having been threatened and nearly attacked by the mob on account of his brother, who is a Captain in the Volunteer Cavalry.'[12]

John Wishaw had entered the school in 1776. After graduating from Trinity College, Cambridge, he was called to the Bar, became a Commissioner for auditing public accounts and a Fellow of the Royal Society. He also frequented Holland House, the great Whig political, literary and artistic centre, where Sheridan, Moore and Macaulay were among the guests and where he hobnobbed with the great Whigs of the day. Sidney Smith described him as 'one of the most sensible men in England, and his opinions valuable if he will give them'. Not all shared his view of the man nicknamed the Pope of Holland House. A cooler assessment was that 'he is a d - d old humbug; dines at Holland House'.[12]

The post-war fall in prosperity affected most areas of the community. By 1817, the numbers at the school had fallen to thirty boarders and nineteen day scholars and were to fall still further. Dr Davies' salary at the time was £200 'and a spacious house, clear of taxes', while fees were five guineas for entrance, thirty-five to forty guineas a year for board and education, and one guinea a quarter for dancing, fencing and drawing.[13] By now, the governors were starting to find the 1774 Act's stipulations regarding the leasing of school property rather restrictive and in 1824 obtained a second Private Act. Its main and rather dubious feature was that it enabled the governors to lease out land for up to 999 years.

The 1820s were turbulent years for Macclesfield. The population had doubled since 1801. Periods of temporary relief alternated with disastrous slumps; there were panics and riots. Such was the tension and disaffection that Sir Walter Scott, staying in the town in November 1826, was strongly advised by the people at his inn not to travel at night.[14] Crime, professional, casual and juvenile increased sharply and, for the poor, living conditions were unspeakable. With a total absence of sewers and no official responsibility for the disposal of human and animal waste, filth piled up in the courtyards and open drains in the streets. But, for those who did have money, there were plenty of places to spend it. The 236 retail shops listed in Macclesfield in 1825 included, among the usual bakers, grocers and drapers, five booksellers, twenty-six tailors and a portrait painter.[15]

It may not only have been the decline in prosperity that caused the slump in numbers at the school in Dr Davies' last years. The Charity Commissioners' Report[16] was not without its criticisms: 'Writing, arithmetic, geography, mathematics and French have been taught in the school, but no instruction has been given in any modern language except French, nor have any new branches of science ... been introduced.' Other things were preying on his mind, too. In 1826, less than two years before his death at the age of 73, he was deeply troubled by a scandal which received national coverage: the Wakefield abduction case.

In Paris, Dr Davies' daughter Frances had married a widower much older than herself. One of her two stepsons, the attractive and talented Edward Gibbon Wakefield, held a post at the British Embassy there but found his income wholly inadequate for his lifestyle. A wealthy bride seemed the easiest way of acquiring an infusion of capital. Frances, as it happened, knew of a likely candidate, tucked away in the hills close to her old home: Ellen Turner, only child of William Turner of Shrigley Hall, a wealthy retired cotton spinner and High Sheriff of the County of Chester. She was only sixteen.

A plan was hatched. The Wakefield brothers drove to Ellen's school in Liverpool and convinced her that her mother was seriously ill and they had been sent to fetch her. Once she had been persuaded into their carriage, they drove her to Gretna Green, where she was induced to go through a marriage ceremony with Edward, and the party fled to France.

If the Wakefields thought that William Turner's main concern would be to hush the matter up, they were mistaken. The family was made of sterner stuff. Armed with a warrant for the

Wakefields' arrest, Ellen's uncle and a Macclesfield lawyer, together with a Bow Street runner, crossed the Channel, discovered the party at Calais and brought them home. The brothers were tried and sentenced to three years in prison but Frances Wakefield escaped judgment as it was decided that she had taken no actual part in the abduction.

It required a special Act of Parliament to annul the marriage. Two years later, Ellen Turner married Thomas Legh of Lyme but died in childbirth in 1831. She was barely twenty-one. Edward Gibbon Wakefield was more fortunate. Having served his sentence, he devoted himself to becoming an authority on the colonies and his contributions were such that a plaque to his memory was placed in the Colonial Office. Frances Wakefield and her husband lived for many years at Great Oak Farm in Sutton, which she inherited from her mother. She and her father, Dr Davies, both lie buried in Prestbury Churchyard.[17]

# Chapter Eight
*'Extending the Benefits
of the Institution'*

At the end of George IV's reign some vigorous new blood was needed to revive the school from its depressed state at the time of Dr Davies' death. The man who was to guide the school successfully through the reign of William IV to the threshold of the Victorian era came from one of Macclesfield's more distinguished families. Son of the Park Green doctor and former mayor, the Revd Francis Stonehewer Newbold was not, however, the first choice to succeed Dr Davies. In January 1828, on Dr Davies' death, the second master, Joseph Cooke, took over as acting head and, in October, the Revd Thomas Bourdillon was elected. He lasted only a few months before resigning.

In his place came Francis Newbold, fellow of Brasenose College and owner of Foden Bank in Sutton. He operated an interesting form of entrance test to the school: 'Boys are not considered eligible to enter ... who are unable to write a sentence from The Spectator, dictated by the Master, without gross orthographical errors.'[1] While Newbold was working to re-establish the school's academic reputation and reverse the trend of declining numbers, the governors were giving radical thought to the school's future direction.

Though 'modern subjects' had been officially introduced into the curriculum by the 1774 Act, their role had always been subordinate. The governors recognised that the steadily increasing demand from a new, articulate middle class was for an education with a more commercial and technical bias, but they were reluctant to alter the essentially classical character of the school. Their answer to the dilemma, proposed in 1834, was to establish two separate schools, thus 'extending the Benefits of the Institution'.[2]

One would be the old Grammar School, which would retain its traditional bias, under a headmaster at £300 per annum and an usher at £160. The other would be a Modern School, to be built nearby, where writing, arithmetic, mathematics and modern languages would be taught. The Modern School headmaster would be paid £130 per annum and his assistant £50. French and Writing Masters, each paid £60, would attend both schools. The headmaster of the Grammar School would be overall head of both schools and both would be under the same governing body. Authorisation for the establishment of the 'Modern Free School' came four years later in a Private Act of Parliament in July 1838.

Meanwhile, in June 1832, the House of Lords had finally, reluctantly, passed the Reform Bill and Macclesfield was at last enfranchised. The town's first brace of MPs were both educated at the school: the Liberal John Brocklehurst and the Tory John Ryle. There were other local excitements that decade. The Macclesfield Canal, constructed by Thomas Telford, opened for traffic in 1831; so, four years later, did the New Buxton Road, which passed through the Hallefield estate owned by the school. A Watch Committee was set up to appoint constables, and a long-overdue act was passed regulating the town's water supply. The improvements to the drainage system came too late, however, to protect the townspeople against the cholera epidemic of 1832. The poor, especially, suffered appallingly.[3]

Macclesfield was by now regarded as the country's leading centre of silk manufacture and silk production was embarking on a period of vigorous growth. The school, too, was in a very healthy state financially. In 1836 the governors founded an Exhibition 'to be held at either University'. The very first Exhibitioner was George Brodrick, who had already scooped up prizes for distinction in the half-yearly examinations (three sovereigns for Grammar, Philology and Translations, two sovereigns for Euclid and Algebra, four sovereigns for being first in the examinations). Tragically, he was killed on his way to take up his place at Brasenose College when his coach overturned near Banbury. He is buried at Deddington, Oxford.[4]

In 1837, the year that the young Queen Victoria came to the throne, Francis Newbold resigned on the grounds of poor health, stating that he was 'intending to try his constitution for a few years in the East'.[5] The move obviously worked, for he lived another forty years. The school governors at the time were Davies Davenport, Lawrence Wright, John Ryle MP, Thomas Legh, Sir Edward Strachey, Revd John Darcey, John

Baskervyle Glegg, William Turner, MP, Revd Charles Thorneycroft, Thomas Ryle Daintry, William Hopes, Henry Dixon, Revd W Cruttenden and the Revd Thomas Mawdsley.

The new headmaster, the Revd William Osborne of Trinity College, Cambridge, was to remain at the school for twelve years. Building on Newbold's foundations, by 1844 he had increased the number of pupils to sixty, with five assistant masters, and was pressing the governors to extend and improve the school: 'The character of a school in these days, suffers by the opinion which educated visitors form of it and the unanimous opinion of all mine has been that we shall never do much without more showy and effective premises.'[6] The school would eventually get such premises but not until after Osborne had left to take up the headship of Rossall School.

Osborne held - for the time - rather advanced views on corporal punishment. In 1839 Charles de Hay, the French master, was called to account for over-zealous discipline. He did not trouble to deny the abuses, merely commenting, 'Reform - *c'est impossible*.' Five years later, the usher, Mr Bennett, was summoned before the governors because of 'the excess of his punishments and denying the Head Master's right of interference'.[7] The boys doubtless agreed with their headmaster that reform in this area was highly desirable. There were also other matters that they felt strongly about. On 12th October 1838, they had written to the governors on an important issue:

'We beg the favour of you to request Mr Osborne to grant us an additional fortnight to our Christmas holidays and we beg of you to take into your consideration the shortness of the Vacation as it is at present fixed. The holidays at Rugby are eight weeks at Christmas, and we believe at other Public Schools they are the same. We venture, therefore, to request this favour, and hope you will not think us unreasonable.'[8]

Other questions preoccupied the governors that autumn. The passing in July of the Private Act had allowed them to proceed with plans for the Modern Free School and they were pondering the purchase of a suitable site. In December they sold property in Chester to the Chester & Crewe Railway Company for £4,566.3s.4d and, the following year, bought various parcels of land in Macclesfield. Included in these was a plot bounded by Great King Street and Bridge Street - the site for the Modern School.

Building work began in 1840 but, much to the annoyance of the townspeople, completion was repeatedly delayed by the high costs. The first Modern School headmaster, Revd H Oram, formerly of St John's College, Cambridge, was not elected until March 1844. Benjamin Turner was elected first assistant and the school opened quietly in August 1844, with fees at 7s.6d a quarter.

Arguments over an appropriate curriculum for the new school resulted in an astonishingly ambitious list of subjects 'reading, writing, arithmetic, book-keeping, English grammar and composition, geography, history, Scripture history, natural theology, natural philosophy, humanity, algebra, mensuration, land-surveying, trigonometry, French and drawing'[9] - or, as Osborne baldly put it in his 1844 report, 'a plain and practical training for all mechanical employment'. He urges parents to 'consider in which of the two institutions they will wish their children henceforth to be educated'. His own preferences are clear. The Grammar School 'will retain that which is the highest boast and privilege of all English

Grammar Schools, viz: the means of enabling the clever or industrious to rise through the universities or otherwise to the highest positions...'[10]

There were other ventures and new beginnings in Macclesfield at this time. St Paul's Church, recently built on a site donated by the governors of the Grammar School, was consecrated in 1844. The following year saw the opening, with much pomp and circumstance, of the town's first railway. Osborne was among the dignitaries invited to a banquet to celebrate; some of his pupils must have been among the excited crowds who lined the embankment to watch the train leave the station in Beech Lane on its first journey to Manchester.

When, in 1849, Osborne resigned, his letter expressed the hope that he was leaving the school 'with an increased reputation, with more of public confidence'. He was also, he said, leaving it 'with a library of 600 or 700 volumes'.[11] Did that library contain any of the great works of the early Victorian period? Would the boys have had an opportunity to read *Oliver Twist, Nicholas Nickleby, Jane Eyre, Wuthering Heights* or *Mary Barton?* They had all appeared in print while Osborne was in office. Two of them highlighted conditions in the very worst sort of schools and sharpened an already active public interest in educational matters.

The available schooling in Macclesfield had expanded dramatically in the previous twenty years. There were now twenty-four private schools, together with a number of elementary schools set up by local churches and chapels for those who could not afford high fees,[12] while the Society for the Diffusion of Useful Knowledge provided opportunities for further education. In the next decade a ragged school for the poorest children of the town would be started by a group of young men from the new St Paul's Church, under the guidance of their vicar, Henry Briant.[13]

It was from a new, but decidedly not ragged, school in the south that the Revd Thomas Brooking Cornish came to replace Osborne. After gaining a first class in Greats and a fellowship at Oriel College, he had gone as an assistant master to Marlborough College, which opened in 1843. Like Osborne, he was faced in Macclesfield with one or two members of staff whose ideas on corporal punishment belonged more to Lowood

School than to the modern, enlightened, mid-nineteenth century establishment which Cornish aspired to lead. The usher, Rhodes, for one, 'made too frequent and improper use of the cane … and assumed a position of independence and disregard of the authority of the Head Master'. Rhodes had to go.[14]

The separation of the Grammar and Modern Schools grieved Cornish, as it was to grieve his pupil and later successor, Darwin Wilmot. He was strongly in favour of reuniting the two schools but, though he lived to be ninety, he did not quite see the fulfilment of his wish. He was consoled, however, by the Grammar School's move in 1855 to its third and present home, when he became the school's first headmaster to be given a house away from the school site. The house was in Westbrook Street and Cornish considered the move there as one of the happiest moments of his life.[15]

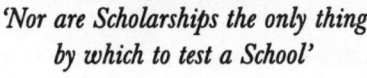

## Chapter Nine

*'Nor are Scholarships the only thing by which to test a School'*

Macclesfield in the 1850s was flourishing. The silk boom would continue until brought to an abrupt end in 1860 by the Free Trade Treaty,[1] and the town was also developing as a shopping centre. As well as over 800 shops, it boasted fifteen surgeons, eleven firms of lawyers, three 'Professors of Music', two coach builders and, significantly, nine pawnbrokers. Its population in 1851 was just under thirty thousand; its thirst was slaked by 122 inns and forty-two beer houses.

On the outskirts of the town was the land earmarked for the new Grammar School buildings. Realising the limitations of the King Edward Street site, the governors had drawn up proposals, approved by the Court of Chancery in 1854, for the school's move to its present home. The Court also approved the relocation of the headmaster's residence to Westbrook House and the teaching of more modern subjects, including chemistry and physical science, drawing and designing.

The new site adjoined open countryside. Westminster Road, Cumberland Street and the Infirmary did not yet exist; Coare Street was only half its present length. As well as the school, there was to be a house for the second master 'so as to ensure at all times effective control and supervision over the Scholars',[2] and a porter's lodge. Work began in October 1854. The town water supply was installed but, although gas had been available in Macclesfield since 1818, the governors resolved 'that no gas is at present to be conveyed to the new School buildings'.[3] Oil lamps were used instead. A cricket field, cut in two by the road from the lodge, was constructed on the site of the present front field.

In 1855, while Britain was anxiously following the progress of the Crimean War, the school moved into the building that is now the library. The house in King Edward Street survived for another seventy years, only to be demolished to make way for extensions to a bus station. Its Queen Anne staircase was re-used in a London mansion;[4] some of its oak beams went to make the long table which is still in the Alan Cooper Library today.

One of the first pupils on the new site was Darwin Wilmot, a future headmaster. He boarded with the Revd Cornish at Westbrook House and his memories of the school are happy. He recalls excellent teaching in Classics, a cricket XI which 'depended too much on the Old Boys' and masters who were liked and respected.

Out of school, paper-chases and pole-jumping were popular with the boys and in the summer holidays there were cricket matches against village clubs. Those with ponies could ride to Eyam, Chatsworth and Castleton. Wilmot's journeys home to Buxton were entertaining: 'There was a coach, not too well horsed, running between Macclesfield and Buxton, and it was quite feasible when going to Buxton to walk to the Cat and Fiddle and arrive there before the coach did.'[5]

The careers of Wilmot's peers at the school show a wide range. As Wilmot was later to remark: 'Nor are scholarships the only thing by which to test a School. That lies more in the way in which the majority of men turn out in after life.'[6] Academic successes were often followed by the church, the law or teaching. The military absorbed some: John Fielden Brocklehurst, later Equerry to Queen Alexandra and Lord Lieutenant of Rutland, took part in the expedition for the relief of General Gordon at Khartoum and was present at the defence of Ladysmith. Others became engineers, like W Clement May who was in charge of part of the Buenos Aires Great Southern Railway, or doctors, architects or bankers.

In 1860 there was a change of headmaster at the Modern Free School. John Chadwick replaced the Revd Oram, who was finding teaching the vast list of subjects with just one full-time assistant almost impossible. Chadwick's approach was more modern and dynamic, placing far greater emphasis on the practical and commercial subjects. The number of pupils increased rapidly: in 1860 there were just eighteen; four years later there were a hundred. Though he stayed at the school for only five years, his successor and first assistant, John Jackson, was cast in a similar mould. Jackson was to run the Modern School for forty successful years.

Work commenced on the town's new infirmary in the 1860s. As with so many other public ventures locally, much of the fundraising was carried out by John May, an old boy of the Grammar School and one of the most influential men in the town. Since the silk trade was suffering from a severe depression at the time, many of the destitute operatives were employed making the foundations of the infirmary and constructing new roads in the area. Cumberland Street and Westminster Road were built, Coare Street, Pownall Street and Brock Street were improved and extended.

The Grammar and the Modern Schools, meanwhile, were being inspected by the Taunton Commission. At the time of the Commission's report in 1868 there were fifty-three day boys and thirteen boarders at the Grammar School and 112 day boys at the Modern School. Though the Commissioners found much to deplore in the state of endowed schools in the country as a whole, the reports on the Grammar and Modern Schools were very satisfactory and both were deemed to compare favourably with their contemporaries. Macclesfield School was the only school in Cheshire to be classed as a first grade Grammar School.[7]

Four years after this achievement, in 1872, the Revd Cornish retired 'in consequence of his failing health'. It was failing less fast than he thought. He lived until 1906, far longer than his successor, Revd A D Gill of Trinity College, Cambridge, who died within a year of taking up the post. The next headmaster, the Revd E Sanderson of Clare College, Cambridge, lasted only a little longer before being dismissed in 1875. Charges against him included giving senior classes 'a number of very broad hints on the set passages in the paper for unseen translation' the day before an examination, over-enthusiastic use of the cane, intemperate language and misleading the Governors.[8]

The scandal affected the school and the governors sought a temporary safe pair of hands to run things while they negotiated a 'New Scheme' with the Charity Commissioners. Once the scheme was agreed, the post would be re-advertised. Darwin Wilmot, former pupil and graduate of Magdalen College, Oxford, was appointed on this understanding but was reappointed unanimously at the end of 1879.

The many requirements of the New Scheme of 1879 included a change to the composition of the governing body; the building of a 'chemical laboratory' and the allowance of more time for modern languages. It was also agreed that the Foundation should give £100 a year towards the education of girls. This was used to help fund the Girls' High School which was established on Park Green in 1880 by the Useful Knowledge Society, with Miss Larrett as headmistress.

By now both schools were providing broadly similar types of education. At the Grammar School, the teaching of Natural Science was increasing from 'early geological classes under Mr Waters to … lectures on Simple Mechanics by Professor Core of Owens College'.[9] One pupil to attend Mr Waters' classes was Arthur Smith Woodward, son of a Macclesfield silk dyer, who won an Exhibition to Owens College. In 1882, he joined the Department of Geology at the British Museum, becoming Keeper in 1901 and returning on at least one occasion to lecture at his old school. A Fellow of the Royal Society, he is now chiefly remembered for his authentication of the Piltdown skull in 1912. When the 'missing link' was eventually exposed as a forgery in the early 1950s, he was thought to be implicated. The recent discovery of a trunk full of bones at the British Museum, however, suggests that the hoax was maliciously engineered by the curator at the time.[10]

Another of Wilmot's pupils with an interest in geology was Hewlett Johnson, who left the school in 1893, won the Geological Prize at Owens College in 1894 and went on to Oxford to read Theology. Dean of Manchester and later of Canterbury, he was an active socialist and would later become famous - or infamous - as the 'Red Dean'. His book *The Socialist Sixth of the World*, was published in 1938 and in 1951 he received the Stalin Peace Prize.

The steady rise in the number of boys and subjects taught at the Grammar School during Wilmot's time necessitated an increase in staff and school buildings. The Modern School, too, was expanding, with the addition of two extra classrooms and a playing field.

As headmaster, Wilmot was held in respect, his moral force admired, his idiosyncrasies cherished: 'In class he made remarks, half aside, of a nature so undiplomatic, so positively indiscreet, as to be only paralleled in some of the famous utterances of the late Lord Salisbury. Of the tact which smooths the way for schoolmasters who have to deal with the fond parents of day boys, he displayed incredibly little.'[11]

When he first arrived, he was warned not to expect to have much say in the management of the school: Hidderley came first, followed by the clerk to the governors, the governors and, finally, the headmaster.[12] Hidderley was the lodge keeper, a cantankerous individual who had been devoted to the Revd Cornish, did not care for Wilmot and 'considered himself an authority on cricket as on everything else'. He neglected the pitch woefully, preferring the role of umpire, and gave some bizarre judgments. A blatant lbw was given not out because 'the boy was batting so prettily that he wanted to see more of his play'.

Other problems beset Wilmot. A minor irritation in 1888 was Mr S E Richards, who set up school in the old house in King Edward Street, calling it the Old Grammar School. Far more seriously, boarders at Wilmot's own house, Westbrook, were struck down that autumn by a mysterious disease which spread through the school. Despite all the attempts at isolation and disinfection, many boys fell seriously ill and one died. Eventually it was diagnosed as scarlet fever but meanwhile there was sensational and sometimes adverse coverage in the press.

The school recovered to enjoy the last decade of the century and Queen Victoria's Diamond Jubilee. Cricket matches against other schools became an annual fixture and a gymnasium was built. In London, Henry Wood conducted his first Queen's Hall Prom and *The Importance of Being Earnest* had its opening performance. In Macclesfield a new school orchestra was organised and plays as such as *A Sheep in Wolf's Clothing* and *Husband to Order* were staged in the new gymnasium. Presumably they fulfilled Wilmot's exacting criteria for pieces 'which are not too ambitious, nor so long as to take time from the School work, which have no innuendoes or jokes of a doubtful nature, and the characters of which … are within the acting powers of an average Cheshire boy with an average Cheshire accent.'[13]

## Chapter Ten
### 'The past four years will never be forgotten'

Change was in the air. It was a new century and there would shortly be a new monarch. For the school, about to celebrate its four hundredth anniversary, the changes proposed by the Board of Education were not always welcome. Darwin Wilmot approved of the decision in 1900 that the County Council should send scholars to the school but he was indignant that an institution which 'had won so many open Scholarships and other Honours in proportion to its numbers'[1] should not otherwise be left in peace.

The Board had other ideas. For a short time, the school was made a centre for pupil teachers, a scheme which worked well, with the pupil teachers integrating successfully and playing for the football and cricket teams. In 1904 a team of inspectors arrived to advise on management and to decide if the school was eligible for a grant, in line with the Royal Commission on Secondary Education's recommendations in 1895. Though

Wilmot may have resented the intrusion, one of the inspectors' conclusions reinforced what he had long been arguing for: that the Grammar and Modern Schools should be reunited. Less well received were their recommendations on the syllabus. Wilmot felt that there had been plenty of changes already, 'all of them tending to increase the time given to the Modern-side subjects and to lessen the time given to Classics'.[1]

While the governors debated what direction the school should take ideologically, the Girls' High School moved physically. In 1909 it left its first home on Park Green for a new building on the site of Charles Brocklehurst's house, The Fence. The new headmistress was Miss Sophie Adams.[2] At the Grammar School, the number of Exhibitions was increased by a bequest of £1,000 from F D Brocklehurst of Hare Hill, whose brother, T U Brocklehurst of Henbury Hall, had been similarly generous twenty years earlier. Macclesfield, meanwhile, was enjoying a new technology: *The World Famous New Parisian Electric Life Motion Pictures* at the Opera House. In London, there was the excitement of the Olympic Games, which were staged in Britain for the first time. The lacrosse team was captained by Mason, an old boy of the school.

In 1910, the year of Wilmot's retirement, the governors at last made up their minds. The Grammar and Modern Schools would be amalgamated on the site of the Grammar School, and the buildings, laboratories and playing fields extended accordingly. Westbrook House would be sold, the second master's house would become the headmaster's residence, more entrance scholarships would be granted and the scope of the Foundation would be widened.[3]

The man chosen to lead the school through this demanding period was Francis Duntz Evans, a graduate of Brasenose College and formerly a master at Merchiston Castle, Edinburgh. A pupil described him as 'a distinguished classical scholar and a brilliant, if forceful teacher ... In appearance he resembled Elgar, in style he was patrician, in politics Conservative, and in manner Ciceronian.'[4]

The task that confronted him was no easy one. He had to weld together a Grammar School, proud of its ancient traditions, and a larger Modern School with its own excellent reputation as a commercial academy. Two hundred boys had to be reconciled to the new situation and new buildings put up. Over twenty years later, the way he rose to the challenge was remembered: 'We measured Mr Evans' success at the start by the immediate disappearance of every trace of jealousy and the instant consciousness ... that we were invited and expected to assist in making Macclesfield once more a name that counted among the country schools of England.'[5] Evans was greatly helped by the able and loyal Edgar Tadman, who had replaced John Jackson as headmaster of the Modern School and who now became deputy headmaster of the Grammar School.

The new buildings were finished in the summer term of 1912 and officially opened by the Bishop of Chester in July. Boarding facilities were still offered with the assistant masters at £50 a year; tuition fees were £3 a term for boys aged twelve and over and £2 a term for boys under twelve. The minimum age of admission was eight years;[6] it would not be reduced to seven until 1950. The Modern School, though closed, was not forgotten. Thanks to a fund set up by its old boys, a reference library was founded in its name.

With the school safely established in its new buildings, Evans was able to turn his attention to those boys who could not afford the cost of higher education. At an Old Boys' Reunion Dinner in 1913, he suggested the establishment of 'a loan fund, from which the boys who wanted to go to other institutions after leaving School, should be able to borrow, and then pay back in their own time.'[7]

No-one at that dinner could have predicted the horrors that the young men under discussion would be facing over the next few years. The First World War claimed the lives of some seventy old boys from the school. Among those who died was Horace Arthur Seel, School Captain 1913-14. He was just nineteen years old when he was killed at Gallipoli in December 1915, having joined the 7th Cheshires in 1914 after his first term at Oxford. Within seven months the School Captain 1912-13, Roy Mellor, was also dead, killed in action in France. Edgar Tadman, the deputy head, was another to join up at the start of the war. On his farewell visit to the school, 'he was greeted with hearty cheers, the whole School afterwards going down to the Station to see him off'.[8]

*Part of the 1855 building, now library and offices*

*The war memorial and cricket pavilion*

By the end of 1916, the slaughter on the Somme was dragging to a close, with the British Army's dead and injured totalling 420,000. The following spring, the School Magazine was doing its best to remain cheerful, recording 'Meatless Days, War Loan, Paper Shortage, Tribunals, non-Theatricals ...'[9] In April the school received a letter from Mr M, one of three masters who, together with all the prefects, were called up that year:

'I was at Rouen training for a fortnight and then came up the line ... On arrival I found my company had just lost all its officers save the captain and most of its men in a raid the Huns had made on them a few days before ... We lived in the support trenches for three days - quite comfy save for the mud. That was knee deep in places and occasionally my men stuck and had to be hauled out by ropes ... After a night in the open we were turned for a time into a working battalion and made railways and roads for a fortnight. We moved a lot, doing this from village to village, and the thoroughness of the destruction was nothing short of marvellous. Not a pail or a bowl was there in the refuse without a hole in it - every tree was lopped down ... and not a house left standing ... Times have been rather hard lately - two hours sleep in 48 hours, and heavy snow with no blankets, but we hope to be in rest soon.'[10]

The summer term 1917 wore on, with much patriotic digging of the school's potato patch. At least one old boy at the Front, ACL, was thinking wistfully of Macclesfield.

'Out here one's mind often wonders how people are at home. I suppose there is the usual talk about Barnaby now, and everyone will be holiday making. I am with the same battalion that A McK was with, and on the whole am having a pretty good time ... Last night we had a stunt on the front line and I was second in command of the company for the night ... The trench we were in has not been in our hands very long, only a few days, and really its sides are practically built up of dead Boches and filled in with soil. The smell is terrible and now I carry Eau de Cologne on my handkerchief for future occasions ... I had rather a narrow escape the other night. I was putting up some wire entanglements when a shell burst only five yards from me. I flung myself down on the wire, and how the shell missed me was a miracle. In getting up again I managed to rip my breeches pretty well, but as everyone says here, "C'est la guerre." I shall be glad to have a letter from anyone at school who cares to write.'[10]

When the guns at last fell silent on 11th November 1918, three-quarters of a million men from Britain, and another 200,000 from the empire, had died. The School Magazine that Christmas sadly recorded the passing of many old boys and promised a welcome to those who returned: 'We assure them all of our gratitude and we must make them feel that the past four years will never be forgotten.'[11]

The Peace Celebrations took place the following July and the school took part in the town's procession of scholars. The feasting was limited by food shortages but a free tea was provided, 'value eightpence nominal, calculated by the Food Authorities to furnish the maximum number of calories per unit mass'.[12] Three masters had returned from the war, Mr Tadman, Mr Mason and Mr Davies, and by the autumn term the school was fully staffed once more.

Numbers went up and in 1921 an extra form had to be housed in the Parish Church Institute opposite the school gates. By the mid 1920s the average number of pupils was 350, including an annual entry of about twenty-five Cheshire County scholarship boys. The old gas lighting was replaced by electricity and the school began to wear an air of prosperity again after the deprivations of the war years.

The School Magazine carried on faithfully recording events. In the summer of 1921 it reported the untimely death of an old boy who was a brilliant naturalist and early conservationist: Charles Gordon Hewitt, Entomologist and Consulting Zoologist in Canada. A happier event, in 1923, was the headmaster's marriage in Scotland. In 1924 the magazine mused on the recent spate of elections and changes of government. A Sixth Former, GW, contributed a pithily relevant poem:

'All parties declare without reservation
The undoubted value of sound education
But in what education precisely consists
Is shrouded in grey, hypothetical mists.'[13]

The introduction of hockey as a school game was recorded in the magazine in 1925, and rugby football in 1928. The latter would soon replace soccer as the school's winter game. Further generous legacies to the school were reported, one from Col W B Brocklehurst, the other from an old boy, Mr Arthur Horsfield.

An important ceremony in Francis Evans' final years at the school was the unveiling and dedication of the War Memorial Tablet in May 1929. Four years later he retired, having led the school with great commitment and ability for twenty-three years. His going was mourned:

'None of us has known the School without Mr Evans and it is difficult to imagine what it will be like when he has gone. We have heard the School described as the happiest in the North of England and, without any undue spirit of self-righteousness, we feel that this may well be true.'[14]

# Chapter Eleven

*'A reputation for educational experiment and advance'*

Thomas Taylor Shaw - 'T T' as he became known - was 32 when he took over from Francis Evans. It was 1933, the year after scientists in Cambridge discovered the neutron and split the atom, the year before Sir Oswald Mosley called for a fascist dictatorship. The school had a population of 429 boys when the new headmaster, a mathematics scholar from Balliol and a rugby enthusiast, arrived from Cheltenham College. Years later he recalled his first impressions:

'Coming as I did from one of the more select and decorous of England's Public Schools, I experienced an almost agonising feeling of claustrophobia as I was swirled along the top corridor in an apparently irrestistible ebb and flow of humanity which showed scant respect for my archimagisterial person ... I found, and still find ... that the boys were far from servile. The "Yes, Sir! No, Sir!" attitude ... has never shown signs of taking hold here.'[1]

His recognition of the distinctive nature of his new material and his success in handling it were reflected in steadily rising numbers. He told old boys at a reunion dinner in 1935 that things were going well: 'Do not infer from this that the boys never do anything wrong, or are perfect. I should begin to think there was something radically wrong if this were to happen, but with regard to things that really matter, the school is in a very healthy state.'[2]

The Old Boys' Association had been revived that year, having previously long flourished under Dr J B Hughes, and a project very close to its heart came to fruition in September.[3] At a special ceremony, the war memorial library and cricket pavilion were opened by Sir William Bromley-Davenport, chairman of the governors. After the First World War, a fund had been set up but the income was initially used to help the sons of old boys who had died. When this was no longer needed, work began on the building, which was designed by F C Sheldon. Over the verandah is engraved: 'In Memoriam, 1914-18'.

Fears about another war in Europe were growing while the country settled down to life under

George VI, after the shock of his brother's abdication. In 1938 T T Shaw was elected to the Headmasters' Conference and the school, which had been a direct grant school since 1926, now also became a public school. By Easter 1939 it was no longer calling itself the Macclesfield Grammar School but the King's School, Macclesfield. That year, too, the Junior School became a self-contained entity and took possession of the building which is now the library.

With the outbreak of war came the evacuees. Numbers at the school were nearly doubled by the arrival of 500 boys from Stretford. A complex system for time-sharing the facilities was worked out and additional accommodation was arranged in the 'Tin Tabernacle' opposite the main gates of the school, the Trinity Methodist Chapel and Westbrook House. It was a difficult situation, made worse by an appalling winter. By the end of the spring term 1940, the Stretford schools, like other Manchester schools evacuated to Macclesfield, had returned home.[4] One problem was over but T T Shaw immediately faced another as masters left to join the Forces and replacements had to be found.

In September 1940 the Luftwaffe began to attack Britain's cities. The full horror of the Blitz was brought home to the school that Christmas by the death of the headmaster's wife in a bombing raid on the south coast. The following spring, staff and senior boys began a fire-watching rota, two boys spending the night in the war memorial library and two masters in the staff common room.[5] Help was also required on local farms and the boys went potato picking, learned to drive tractors and spread lime on the newly ploughed Shutlingsloe.[6] By this time, the Rock and part of the lower field had also been ploughed up in the drive to produce more food.

After a despondent silence for over two years, the Macclesfield church bells rang out on 7th November 1942 to celebrate the victories in the Middle East. It was believed that the tide had at last turned. Regaining lost ground was slow and painful but by October 1944 an old boy was able to write from Holland, where he had visited a newly liberated town:

'The whole town was drunk with wine and joy, British and Dutch flags everywhere ... Dense crowds cheering as each tank came into view, flowers thrown from balconies and all this where the Wehrmacht held sway only 24 hours before.'[7]

Nearly 300 Old Boys and nine masters served in the Forces during the war. Forty or more lost their lives and many were decorated. Tribute was paid to them in the School Magazine: 'When we leave this school and go into the world, let us pledge ourselves to do everything to ensure that their lives have not been sacrificed in vain.'[8] Those who had died were given a permanent memorial in the magnificent wrought iron gates at the entrance to the school, thanks to the Old Boys' Association.

While the country adjusted to peace, the governors had to decide whether to adopt maintained voluntary status or return to full independence, the 1944 Education Act having cast doubt on the future of direct grant schools. After pressure from the Government and Cheshire County Council, they chose full independence and the school left the direct grant list in 1946. The financial blow was softened by an arrangement with the County Council, who agreed to purchase places at the school for boys who had passed their 11+ examination. The Council now decided the school's

*The approach to the Coarse Street bridge from the Pool*

*The Main School building*

catchment area and selected 90% of those pupils who obtained free places.

The decade ended with a flat being added to the first floor of the headmaster's house, freeing the ground floor for classrooms and offices, while the first new building of the 1950s was a dining hall. One old boy recalls meals in the old dining room, where the master or prefect at the end of each long table carved the roast,[9] and the School Magazine regretted that one would 'no more hear the traditional Prefect's Grace and the ensuing scrape of chairs on the wooden floor of the old Dining Room, no more eat and talk under the quiet beneficent eye of Raphael's Sistine Madonna'.[10]

In celebration of Queen Elizabeth II's coronation in 1953, each boy in the school was given a gilt medallion by the governors and a silk handkerchief by the Macclesfield Silk Traders' Association. The year before there had been excitement over the success of an old boy, Peter Forbes Robinson, who won the Mario Lanza Competition and went on to study at La Scala. As a member of the Royal Opera Company, he was to take many leading roles and in 1962 created the title role in Tippett's *King Priam* for the Coventry Festival.

The remainder of T T Shaw's headmastership saw a flurry of building to accommodate the rapid increase in numbers from around 740 in the early 1950s to over a thousand by the end of the decade. Beech Lane Methodist Sunday School was hired as an interim classroom and a new Art Block was built, named after the Duchess of Kent who opened it in 1957. Two science laboratories followed in 1958. A serious fire in 1959 meant that the assembly hall had to be rebuilt; at the same time the library was moved to its present site and a new block built in the garden of the headmaster's flat.[11] Until their new premises on the Rock were completed in 1962, the Juniors were temporarily housed in the Trinity Sunday School.

In 1966, after leading the school in his own inimitable, individual and highly successful style for thirty-three years, T T Shaw retired. During his time the school had expanded greatly and acquired 'a reputation for educational experiment and advance, paralleled by the development of a lively musical tradition and prowess on the sports field'.[12]

His replacement was Alan Cooper, formerly Head of Mathematics at Dulwich College and a mathematics scholar and rugby Blue from Queen's College, Oxford. On his arrival, in the year that England triumphed over its World Cup win and grieved over the appalling loss of life at an Aberfan primary school, he was confronted with a major challenge. The school, now with a population of over 1200, was not only seriously overcrowded but also faced the possibility that the County Free Places scheme would be axed. Comprehensive schools were becoming the preferred option for local authorities.

A major development programme was set in motion. The construction of the Coare Street footbridge in 1968 was followed by the completion the next year of the Rock Block, giving much needed classroom space and a Sixth Form Common Room. The Percyvale Science Block was built on the site of the Pearl Street Dyeworks in 1976, and in 1983 the nineteen-acre playing fields, named after Lord Derby, were opened. In 1983, too, after years of living above the school, the headmaster was provided with a more spacious home in Alderley Road, next to the Derby Fields.

Throughout this time, King's was going from strength to strength academically, in the performing and visual arts and in sport. Old boys were distinguishing themselves in all fields. Sir Tony Wrigley was pursuing the remarkable academic career which would eventually culminate in his becoming Master of Corpus Christi College, Cambridge. Alan Beith, who left the school in 1961, was elected Liberal MP for Berwick-upon-Tweed in 1973. In the arts, Bruce Myers, at the school until 1960, was starting to make his name in some of Peter Brook's productions at the Bouffes-du-Nord Theatre in Paris, and in 1974 Christian Blackshaw won first prize in the Alfredo Casella International Piano Competition. In sport, S J Smith, as England's scrum-half, surpassed by four the record of twenty-four caps held by Jeeps, and was captain of the England XV from 1981-3 and the British Lions in 1983, while F Millett was for many years a cornerstone of Cheshire cricket and captain of the Minor Counties XI.

Meanwhile, protracted negotiations were still taking place with Cheshire County Council regarding the County Free Places. Despite an agreement in 1975 for a phased reduction to 25%, the

Council came under political pressure to terminate the arrangement in 1979 and the school had to prepare for its first completely fee-paying intake. The new Government Assisted Places Scheme, however, promised some help to those who could not afford full fees and the first pupils under the scheme were admitted to the school in 1981.

Alan Cooper's twenty-one years at the school ended, as they had begun, with a major challenge: the admission of girls to the Sixth Form. Twenty-five arrived in September 1986, the start of a highly successful initiative and the spearhead of further radical changes. On his retirement the following July, the governors paid a warm tribute to his inspired leadership. In recognition of his 'outstanding contribution to the development of the school',[13] the school library, which had been extensively remodelled, was named The Alan Cooper Library.

# Epilogue
### 'This mysterious personality
### of a school'

When the school was a mere 250 years old -
only half its present age - it was starting to
feel the first ripples of the Industrial Revolution.
Now, at the end of the twentieth century, it is
experiencing the effects of a worldwide Information Technology revolution, whose significance
may well prove even greater. It is against this
background that King's present headmaster has
presided over a major reorganisation of the
school.

An exhibitioner of Jesus College, Oxford,
Adrian Silcock arrived in 1987 from Southamp-
ton, where he was Senior Master and Head of
Modern Languages at King Edward VI Grammar School. He joined a school which, apart from
its recent intake of girls into the Sixth Form, was
still very much a traditional boys' school. A feeling prevailed that single-sex education, so long
successful, should be continued for pupils aged
11-16, but it was also felt to be anachronistic that

*The Junior Division*

*The Girls' Division*

younger girls should be denied the benefits of the school. The decision was taken to make the Junior Division co-educational and to create a new Girls' Division. With the Sixth Form and Boys' Division, there would be four separate and highly distinctive Divisions.

The process began in 1992 with the purchase of the old Macclesfield High School for Girls in Fence Avenue. The buildings had been empty for some time but were rapidly transformed into spacious and attractive accommodation and the Girls' Division opening ceremony in September 1993 was a pleasing reaffirmation of the links that had existed with the High School since 1880. In October, the Bishop of Doncaster opened the Junior Division's new premises. Within four years, these had expanded to include an Infants' Department. Planning for the future has not ended there. With the greater space available at Cumberland Street, an Appeal has been set up to raise funds for a new Sixth Form centre, drama studio and sports hall.

Such enterprise and vigour are typical of a school which has survived triumphantly for nearly five hundred years. Building on its experiences,

King's has developed that 'mysterious personality of a school [which] is the product of all the generations that have passed through it'.[1] It is a very individual and pleasing personality, for the school has evolved into a lively, successful and tolerant establishment, bubbling with new ideas, its open-minded approach underpinned by ancient traditions. With a commitment to academic excellence and a distinguished staff, it produces a great many academic high flyers but is also prepared to spend time helping less brilliant pupils fulfil their potential. It is, as the government inspectors reported, 'a very caring community'.

It is also a community humming with activity. King's is justly renowned for its plays, concerts and art exhibitions which attract audiences from a wide area. It produces national and county sports players almost as a matter of course and its outstanding reputation has recently been confirmed by the conferral of the Sports Council's Sportsmark Gold Award.

As Darwin Wilmot said, part of the test of a school is the way in which its pupils turn out in later life. Countless pupils have passed through the school since it was founded by Sir John

Percyvale in 1502. Some have achieved great distinction; many more, mostly now forgotten, have made their contribution to society away from the limelight. All have played their part in making the King's School in Macclesfield the vibrant place it is today, a school inextricably linked with the town whose development and history it has shared for so long. May both long continue to flourish.

# Bibliography
# & Chapter Notes

**Byng, J,** *Rides Round Britain* (London: Folio Society, 1996)

**Clegg, J,** *The Diary of James Clegg 1708-55,* Part 3, ed V S Doe (Derbyshire Record Society, 1981)

**Collins, L,** *Macclesfield Sunday School* (Macclesfield Museums Trust, 1996)

**Davies, C S,** *A History of Macclesfield* (Manchester: Manchester University Press, 1961)

**Dore, R N,** *The Civil Wars in Cheshire* (Chester: Cheshire Community Council, 1966)

**Earles, J,** *Streets and Houses of Old Macclesfield,* 1915 (reprinted MTD Rigg Publications, 1990)

**Elton, G R,** *England under the Tudors* (London: Methuen, 1963)

**Hammond, J L & B,** *The Town Labourer* (London: Longman, Green & Co, 1917)

**Hibbert, C,** *The English: A Social History* (London: Grafton Books, 1989)

**Malmgreen, G,** *Silk Town: Industry and Culture in Macclesfield, 1750-1835* (Hull University Press, 1985)

**Maybury, P,** *Golden Days: A Macclesfield Life* (Wilmslow: Sigma Leisure, 1995)

**McGuinness, P,** "The Effect of the Second World War

on the King's School in Macclesfield" (chapter of a thesis for the War Studies Dept, King's College, 1996)

**Myers, A R,** *England in the Late Middle Ages* (London: Penguin, 1991)

**Ormerod, G,** *The History of the County Palatine and City of Chester,* 1819 (reprinted Manchester: E J Morten (Publishers) Ltd, 1980)

**Richards, R,** *The Manor of Gawsworth,* 1957 (reprinted Manchester: E J Morten (Publishers) Ltd, 1974)

**Siggins, G P,** *History of the Old Boys' Association, 1935-85*

**Wilmot, D,** *A Short History of the Grammar School* (Macclesfield: Claye, Brown & Claye, 1910)

**Wilson, E,** *A History of Macclesfield Grammar School in the County of Cheshire* (MEd thesis, 1952)

*For copies of:*

**Sir John Percyvale's will:** see Wilmot, Appendix IV
**William Bridges' will:** see Wilson, Appendix III
**The Charter of King Edward VI:** see Wilmot
**John Bolde's instrument of appointment:** see Wilson, Appendix IIb
**Thomas Brancker's report on the salt mines:** see Wilson, Appendix IVe
**Edward Denham's indictment for murder:** see Wilson, Appendix IVb
**Private Act of Parliament 1774:** see Wilson, Appendix Vd

**Chapter One**

1 Will of Sir John Percyvale
2 See Wilson, pp 2-4
3 Gilbert & Carew, *History of Cornwall* (Wilson, pp 277-8)
4 See Davies, pp 38-39
5 See Wilson, p 12
6 See Wilson, pp 25-26
7 See Davies, p 8
8 See Davies, pp 11-12
9 See Davies, pp 19-20
10 See Davies, pp 40-41
11 See MRH in *School Magazine*, Summer 1967
12 See Wilson, p 5
13 See Davies, p 14
14 See Wilson, p 13
15 See Davies, p 43
16 William Bridges' will
17 See Wilson, p 23

**Chapter Two**

1 See Wilson, p 24
2 See Wilson, pp 8-9
3 See Wilson, p 29
4 Grammar School Papers
5 The Charter of Edward VI
6 See Wilson, Appendix IIa
7 Wilson, pp 35-6
8 John Bolde's instrument of appointment
9 See Davies, pp 305-6
10 William Webb, *The Vale Royal of England*, 1621 (see Ormerod)
11 Articles by Revd Edgar Fripp in *The Hibbert Journal* (see Wilson, p 51)
12 See Wilson, p 51
13 Earwaker, Vol II, pp 260-63
14 School Magazine, Lent 1928

15 Memorial brass in parish church
16 Grammar School Papers
17 See Wilson, pp 55-6
18 See Davies, p 99
19 Capesthorne MS, quoted in Lancs & Ches Antiquarian Society Publications, vol 12
20 See Earles, p 95
21 See Davies, pp 71-2

**Chapter Three**

1 Memorial tablet in parish church
2 Grammar School Papers
3 See Wilson, p 74
4 Malbon, *Memorial of the Civil War* (see Wilson, p 60)
5 See Davies, pp 76-77
6 See Dore, p 28
7 See Wilson, p 62
8 Barlow's *Cheshire*, 1855 (see Wilson, p 61)
9 Earwaker (see Wilmot, p 38)
10 See Wilson, pp 80-85
11 See Wilson p 101
12 See Davies, p 79
13 See Wilson, p 86
14 *Admirable Curiosities, Rarities and Wonders in England, Scotland and Ireland*, 1682 (see Wilson, p 63)
15 See Wilson, p 89
16 Earwaker, p 519
17 See Wilson, p 74
18 Parish church registers (see Wilmot, p 21)
19 Memorial tablet in parish church
20 See Wilson, p 103
21 Grammar School Papers
22 Governors' Minute Book
23 See F E Crowder, *School Magazine*, Spring 1946

24  See Wilson, p 98
25  See Davies, p 80

**Chapter Four**
1   See Wilmot, pp 34-36
2   See Wilson, pp 92-93
3   Grammar School Papers
4   Letter from Bishop of Chester, Nov 1691 (see Wilson, p 78)
5   Governors' Minute Book
6   See Wilson, p 94
7   See Davies, pp 122-3
8   See Malmgreen, p 100
9   See Davies, pp 122-5, and Malmgreen, p 13
10  Governors' Minute Book
11  All details and quotations relating to the Denham case are taken from the copy of his indictment for murder.
12  Governors' Minute Book,
13  Dr Curtis (see Wilson, p 87)

**Chapter Five**
1   See Wilson, p 309
2   See Wilson, p 69
3   See Davies, p 95
4   See Malmgreen, p 5
5   Clegg, pp 923-998
6   See Wilson, pp 124-134
7   Eyewitness account in Earwaker (see Wilson, p108)
8   See Davies, pp106-110
9   Letter dated 14th Dec 1745, from John Stafford, Town Clerk (see Earles, p 27)
10  See Wilson, p110
11  See Wilson, p 13
12  Ormerod, p 742

**Chapter Six**
1   See Earwaker, p 522
2   See Wilson, pp 171-2
3   Macclesfield Corporation minutes (see Davies, p 115)
4   Letter from Sir William Meredith to the Duke of Portland, dated 20 July 1774 (Portland Papers, Nottingham University Library, ref PwF 6744)
5   Byng, p 172
6   See Earles, p 22
7   See Earles, pp 75-6
8   See Malmgreen, pp 145-153
9   Governors' Minute Book
10  Private Act of 1774
11  See Hibbert, p 453
12  Collins, p 7
13  Byng, pp 177-8
14  Grammar School Papers
15  Portland Papers (see 4 above)
16  Earwaker (see Crowder, *School Magazine*, Spr 1946)

**Chapter Seven**
1   See Malmgreen, p 128
2   Ormerod, p 743
3   See Davies, pp 127-8
4   Byng, p 174
5   Byng, p 356
6   See Wilmot, p 30
7   See Wilmot, p 41
8   See Malmgreen, p 137
9   See Wilmot, pp 45-6
10  See Malmgreen, p 52
11  See Malmgreen, p 112
12  See Wilmot, p 32
13  Carlisle, *Endowed Grammar Schools*( see Wilson p 152)
14  See Malmgreen, p 59

15  See Davies, p 167
16  Charity Commissioners' 31ˢᵗ
    Report 1818-37
17  See Earles, pp 36-38

**Chapter Eight**

1  Charity Commissioners'
   Report 1837
2  Governors' Minute Book
3  See Malmgreen, pp 92-6
4  See Wilmot, p 53
5  Governors' Minute Book
6  Grammar School Papers
7  Governors' Minute Book
8  Grammar School Papers
9  Grammar School Papers
10 See Wilson, pp 59-60
11 Grammar School Papers
12 See Davies, p 233
13 See Davies, p 271
14 Governors' Minute Book
15 See Wilmot, p 66

**Chapter Nine**

1  See Malmgreen, p 180
2  Grammar School Papers
3  Governors' Minute Book
4  See R Richards
5  See Wilmot, pp 68-69
6  Wilmot, p 80
7  See Wilson, pp 106 & 221
8  Governors' Minute Book
9  Wilmot, p 91
10 *Daily Telegraph*, 23/5/1996
11 B Leech, *School Magazine*,
   Michaelmas Term 1910
12 See Wilmot, p 110
13 Wilmot, pp 132-3

**Chapter Ten**

1  Wilmot, pp 118-19
2  See Davies, pp 216-7
3  See Wilson, p 255
4  See Wilson, p 256
5  *School Magazine*, Lent 1933
6  School Prospectus, 1911-12
7  *School Magazine*, Lent 1913
8  *School Magazine*, Summer 1915
9  *School Magazine*, Lent 1917
10 *School Magazine*, Summer 1917
11 *School Magazine*, Christmas 1918
12 *School Magazine*, Summer 1919
13 *School Magazine*, Christmas 1924
14 *School Magazine*, Lent 1933

**Chapter Eleven**

1  Speech Day Address, *School
   Magazine*, Summer 1952
2  Undated cutting from *The
   Macclesfield Times*
3  Siggins
4  See McGuinness, pp 23-6
5  See McGuinness, p 46
6  See McGuinness, pp 62-3
7  Letter from CQMS, *School
   Magazine*, Christmas 1944
8  *School Magazine*, Summer 1945
9  Maybury, p 81
10 *School Magazine*, Spring 1951
11 Annual Report, 1959-60
12 Obituary in *Macclesfield Express*,
   17ᵗʰ July 1986
13 Annual Report, 1986-7

**Epilogue**

1  Lord Leverhulme's speech on
   Speech Day 1933, quoting Lord
   Irwin, reported in *The Times and
   East Cheshire Observer*, 4/8/1933

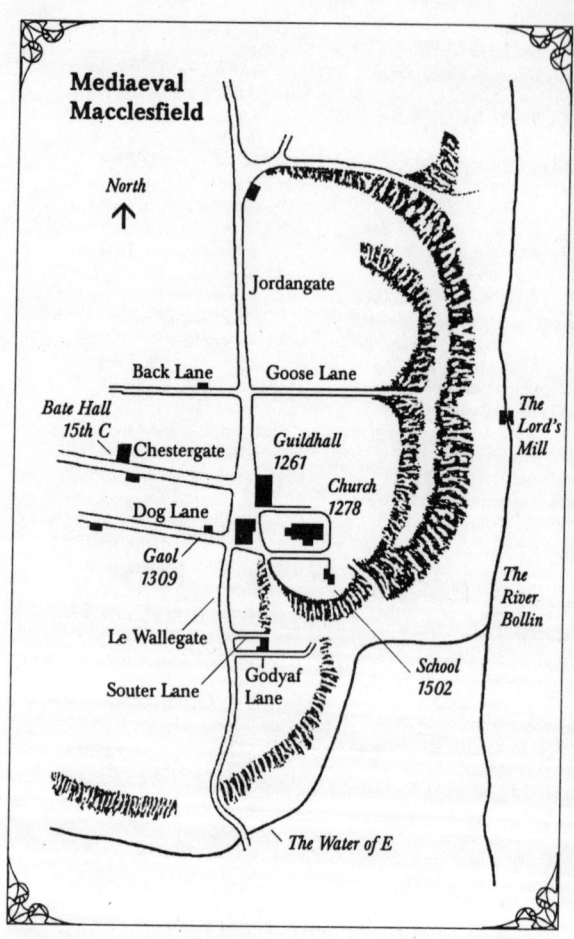

# Mediaeval
# Macclesfield

*North*
↑

Jordangate

Back Lane        Goose Lane

*Bate Hall*
*15th C*     Chestergate        *Guildhall*
                                *1261*
                                        *Church*
                                        *1278*
              Dog Lane

*Gaol*
*1309*

Le Wallegate

Souter Lane        *Godyaf*
                   *Lane*

                              *School*
                              *1502*

*The Water of E*

*The*
*Lord's*
*Mill*

*The*
*River*
*Bollin*